T0271427

Advertising as a Creative Industry

At the crossroads of culture and commerce, the advertising industry is a regime of paradoxes. This book examines the place of advertising in today's creative industries, exploring the major challenges advertisers confront as they engage with other creative sectors. Izabela Derda, author, media scholar, and industry expert, offers insights into how the industry keeps deconstructing its own creative processes and collaborative models as it attempts to stay relevant.

Through extensive case studies and interviews with industry professionals and thought leaders, this book examines the sector's struggle to adapt to new business models and to monetize creativity in today's media landscape, from re-engaging audiences through media more typical of arts and entertainment to managing intricate cross-sectoral creative collaborations. From redesigning workplaces to satisfy the expectations of the youngest generations of creatives to reconsidering the paradigm of conventional creative teams, the advertising sector has swiftly adjusted to the seismic changes in today's media landscape.

The book will be of interest to scholars and students of creative media, advertising, and media studies, as well as those interested in understanding the changing complexities and latest innovations of the creative industries. Advertising professionals, artists, and policymakers will find relevant insights and possible solutions for the major challenges facing the advertising industry today.

Izabela Derda is Assistant Professor in Media & Creative Industries at the Erasmus School of History, Culture and Communication, Erasmus University, the Netherlands. She is also an advertising professional, former head of entertainment at Havas SE, and a jury member for major advertising festivals, such as Cannes Lions or Eurobest.

Routledge Research in the Creative and Cultural Industries

Series Editor: Ruth Rentschler

This series brings together book-length original research in cultural and creative industries from a range of perspectives. Charting developments in contemporary cultural and creative industries thinking around the world, the series aims to shape the research agenda to reflect the expanding significance of the creative sector in a globalised world.

The Venice Arsenal
Between History, Heritage, and Re-use
Edited by Luca Zan

Managing Cultural Joint Ventures
An Identity-Image View
Tanja Johansson, Annukka Jyrämä and Kaari Kiitsak-Prikk

Public Relations as a Creative Industry
Elisenda Estanyol

Co-Leadership in the Arts and Culture
Sharing Values and Vision
Wendy Reid and Hilde Fjellvær

Cultural Work and Creative Subjectivity
Recentralising the Artist Critique and Social Networks in the Cultural Industries
Xin Gu

Advertising as a Creative Industry
Regime of Paradoxes
Izabela Derda

For more information about this series, please visit: www.routledge.com/Routledge-Research-in-the-Creative-and-Cultural-Industries/book-series/RRCCI

Advertising as a Creative Industry
Regime of Paradoxes

Izabela Derda

Routledge
Taylor & Francis Group

LONDON AND NEW YORK

First published 2024
by Routledge
4 Park Square, Milton Park, Abingdon, Oxon OX14 4RN

and by Routledge
605 Third Avenue, New York, NY 10158

Routledge is an imprint of the Taylor & Francis Group, an informa business

British Library Cataloguing-in-Publication Data
A catalogue record for this book is available from the British Library

ISBN: 978-1-032-20301-0 (hbk)
ISBN: 978-1-032-20304-1 (pbk)
ISBN: 978-1-003-26312-8 (ebk)

DOI: 10.4324/9781003263128

Typeset in Times New Roman
by Apex CoVantage, LLC

For Sara

Contents

Acknowledgments   *ix*

Introduction: between cultural and industrial   1

1   Advertising X creativity   13

2   Advertising X innovation   31

3   Advertising X entertainment   50

4   Advertising X other creative sectors   67

5   Advertising: regime of paradoxes   81

    Index   *90*

Acknowledgments

It takes a village to write a book, even a single-authored one, and I am so thankful to all who helped me through this one. To begin with, my deepest thanks go out to Terry Clague—my publisher—for initiating this project in the first place and inviting me to pick up this challenge, which also allowed me to connect my two professional identities: creative industry practitioner and media scholar, and to Naomi Round Cahalin, for making the publishing process smooth and pleasurable. I am also immensely appreciative of Katharine Keenan for making sure that my writing is legible and enjoyable to read, and my student assistants Athina Mitrakou Daki and Paul Hartwig for their assistance in the early stages of developing the draft.

I owe a great debt of gratitude to the people whom I interviewed while conducting research for the book; without their willingness to share their experiences and expertise, this project would not have been possible. I cannot list them all here, but I am equally grateful to those who chose to be identified and those who preferred to stay anonymous.

Moreover, I must express my appreciation to some people who have supported me over the years: Fredda Hurwitz, my role model and mentor during my time at Havas Sports & Entertainment, where I had the pleasure to serve as a Head of Entertainment, as well as all my colleagues there, who always pushed me to strive higher; Dr. Mirosław Filiciak, prof. SWPS—if not for you, I would have dropped my Ph.D. studies and academic path, and I would not be where I am today.

This list would not be complete without mentioning my colleagues from Erasmus School of History, Culture and Communication at Erasmus University in Rotterdam—Prof. Susanne Janssen, Prof. Marc Verboord, Dr. Erik Hitters, and Dr. Tonny Krijnen—thank you for your constant support and trust in me and my ideas!

Last but certainly not least, I must give credit where credit is due to two very important people in life: my husband Łukasz and daughter Sara—for their patience and loving understanding as I embarked on this journey.

This work was supported by the Dutch Research Council (NWO) under Grant KI.18.044.

Introduction

Between cultural and industrial

At the height of the HIV epidemic in the 1980s, Ward 5B at San Francisco General Hospital was the first in the world specifically created and designated to treat patients with the disease. Many of the patients in Ward 5B were already facing prejudice and discrimination in society, but the ward was created as a place of hope and compassion in the face of a devastating illness. The unit's nurses and caregivers emphasized humanity and holistic well-being, creating a new standard of care. The staff treated their patients with dignity and respect, providing not only medical care but also emotional support.

5B is a full-length documentary, directed by two-time Oscar nominee Dan Krauss and Academy Award winner Paul Haggis, which tells the story of the ward.[1] The movie seeks to provide a corrective to the way nurses are often portrayed in pop culture—as assistants to doctors and objects of derision—as these images were having a detrimental effect on society's perception of the nursing profession. It premiered in the main selection in Cannes Film Festival in 2019, next to Almodóvar's *Pain and Glory*, Herzog's *Family Romance, LLC*, and the Oscar-winning Bong Joon-ho's *Parasite*. The film was described as "a moving study in courage and compassion"[2] and "one of the most important documentaries about AIDS ever made".[3] Strikingly, it is also the Grand Prix winner of the advertising industry's equivalent to the Oscar awards: Cannes Lions Festival of Creativity in 2019. With no brand present either in the film's opening credits or anywhere in its 94 minutes duration, it is yet considered one the best advertising works ever created.

There is hardly any industry that fetishizes creativity as much as advertising. From having "creative directors", "chief creative officers", "creative strategists", or even "creative technologists" as central stakeholders and decision-makers in advertising agencies to industry events with "festival of creativity" or "creative circle" in their headings, the sector makes creativity central in everything they do. However, believe it or not, creativity in advertising was not always an obvious connotation. It was definitely not the case prior to the 1960s when the (so-called) Creative Revolution increased the emphasis on creativity and imagination over the formulas and research that had traditionally guided the creation of advertisements,[4] driving the sector's obsession with all things *new* and *different*. Yet today, due to the sector's key focus on

DOI: 10.4324/9781003263128-1

driving revenue and corporate commercial success, persuading the public, and high need for effectiveness, the sector seems to be set somewhat at the periphery of the creative industry, often seen as a kind of impostor among the "true" creative arts invested in creating cultural values.

The tension between commercial principles and cultural values embedded in the concept of creative industries has been a visible concern since their inception in the 1990s. Advertising occupies one of the central roles in this conflict, a hybrid genre that serves as both a persuasive tool aimed at driving sales on the one hand, and a social barometer and a space for cultural critique and creative experimentation on the other hand. As media ecosystems evolve along with major changes in technology, markets, commercial clutter, and consumer expectations, the line between promotional and cultural products is increasingly blurry. Due to the advancing popularity of ad blockers, ad-free streaming platforms, and the fact that audiences are growing more and more critical of advertising, many brands are having difficulty getting access to or engaging with their target markets. As a result, they are looking for new ways to reach consumers by delivering cultural or entertainment value.

For decades, marketers relied on so-called traditional media to convey their commercial messages through outlets such as TV, press, radio, or outdoor, which structured the flow of information and provided the primary venues for paid advertising. This deployment of "push" communication intruded into an audience's time and space, and limited media users' control and agency. With the changes to the media environments of the 21st century, this traditional model is gradually falling apart, and advertising communication is turning toward an invitation- and engagement-based "pull" model,[5] which deliberately follows the autonomous choices of audiences.[6] Recognizing audiences' attention as a valuable resource,[7] companies are seeking ways to depart from traditional modes of communication in order to capture their interest and offer memorable experiences.[8]

Red Bull is a great example. This energy drink brand has been particularly successful in providing quality entertainment content to its customers, converting them from consumers of a product into an almost cult-like fan club of extreme sports and active lifestyles.[9] The success of the brand is partially due to the company's investment in its own professional production company, with offices in Salzburg, Los Angeles, and London, which has produced original programming—from feature-length documentaries to extreme sports events—distributed for free on the Internet and social media sites.[10] The result is a devoted consumer base and an elevation of the brand to category leader.[11]

In a quest to be less ad-like, the advertising industry interacts with various creative sectors, attempting to blend in with numerous forms of culture and entertainment to conceal its persuasive intent. In doing so, the industry rejects its habitual rhetoric by borrowing the aesthetics, formats, and genres of other sectors and deconstructing its former approaches to message development. Therefore, it obscures the basic objective of consumer control, which is ultimately the domain and an imperative of advertising, while contributing to the commodification of attention and reinforcing industry power structures even while claiming to empower individuals.[12]

As advertising evolves new forms in order to hide its persuasiveness, it strives to draw from other creative practices. Hence, the exchange of experiences across sectors and new approaches to marketing communication[13] push advertisers to rethink how they define, create, and distribute brand messages and how audiences consume them.

At the same time, the potential of combining consumer brands with entertainment or cultural experiences seems to be warmly welcomed by representatives on both sides of the arts–advertising divide, who see their marriage as a potential solution to some of their sectors' biggest issues.[14] By uniting in shared dread that digital technologies pose a significant danger to their established business models, the historical animosity and resistance between the sectors has been (at least to some extent) overcome.[15] This shift has had a profound effect not only on the dynamics of creative processes, collaborative working methods, and business models but also on the creative products themselves, as ads are to be found blended into the areas traditionally reserved for cultural products, such as cinemas, museums, or even theaters.[16]

The challenges that today's media environment poses for the advertising sector create new paradigms and dynamics, which demands closer study as they have broad consequences for the sector itself and also for our understanding of advertising as a creative industry. For example, how do these developments affect advertising's comprehending of creativity and innovation today? What implications will these changes have on creative agencies' work processes when it comes to their core functions of delivering creative services? Finally, where does advertising stand amongst other creative industries today?

For whom, on what, and how

The aim of the book, then, is not to preach in favor of the advertising sector nor defend its place within the creative industry. Rather, it investigates the advertising industry's cultural and economic meanings and tensions as it attempts to develop a new identity and engage with other creative sectors, deconstructing its own creative processes and collaborative models. Following the accounts of practitioners, the book examines their discourse as a form of negotiating knowledge and power, and analyzes how actors conceptualize knowledge into practices of common sense regarding how the industry operates. In doing so, the book analyzes how *creativity* and *innovation*—as features ordering affiliation to creative industries, and *cross-sector interchange*—are seen and practiced in today's industry. Hence, the book investigates advertising's position within today's creative sector by looking at the seemingly paradoxical dynamics of the industry's placement at the crossroads of the cultural and commercial by focusing on three notions: (1) advertising's self-identification as creative and innovative at its very core; (2) the industry's continuing exploration of ways to make ads appear less like ads and developing a genre of hybrid messages in their quest for the attention of hyperaware consumers; and (3) the tensions and dynamics within the industry, related to the dual nature of the sector.

The work of this book is deeply attuned to industry practice. It synthesizes (and extensively quotes) accounts from industry professionals and thought leaders, and critically engages with relevant case studies to make sense of the ever-evolving dynamics of the sector. Neither a review of current trends nor a "how to" guide, this book is primarily targeted at scholars and students of creative media, advertising, and media studies, and those who are interested in understanding the changing dynamics and latest complexities of the creative industries. Nonetheless, it will be of interest to advertising professionals, artists, and policymakers, who will gain insights into the major challenges confronting the industry today and hear directly from the innovative practitioners offering solutions. More specifically, their examples encompass how the industry is:

- Monetizing creativity in competitive media and business landscapes and the related need for new business models;
- Re-engaging audiences in a world of content abundance, ad blockers, advertising-restricting platforms, and consumer mistrust through approaches more typically associated with arts and entertainment;
- Attracting and retaining fresh creative talent and establishing creative cultures to satisfy the needs and expectations of the youngest generations of creatives;
- Managing the intricacy of cross-sectoral collaborations and reconsidering the paradigm of conventional creative teams in the advertising sector.

The research on which this book is based combined an analysis of 54 in-depth interviews, which were then expanded through targeted research and discourse analysis on over 200 trade paper publications, policy documents, industry reports, white papers, and publicly available interviews (most coming from vlogs and podcasts). The interviewees for the research were drawn from two groups. The first group is composed of senior figures in creative agencies (including both network and independent agencies) in the capacities of managing directors, executive directors, and creative directors, all of whom were awarded at least once with major industry creativity awards—Cannes Lions, Clio Awards, or Eurobest. The majority are multiaward winners, with 16 of them receiving the Grand Prix award at Cannes Lions at least once during their career, which distinguishes them as experts. The second group is composed of artists, producers and project managers coming from a wide range of other creative sectors that collaborate with the advertising industry (TV, film, music, art, and museum sectors), with experience in contributing to at least three advertiser-initiated projects for commercial brands.

Methodologically, the research adheres to the critical media industries studies approach since it permits examination of the paradoxical conflicts between creative and social expression and the industry's financial and power interests.[17] Through grounded institutional case studies, including an exploration of industry practices, networks, and perceptions, the work examines the connections between broader economic developments and institutional struggles and goals, and the industry practices and discourses in which these are expressed. This approach, while maintaining the detailed and critical perspective of cultural studies, creates a link to the political economy macroview on power relations and adds a critical angle on how the macrodevelopments of the advertising industry are negotiated within the industry itself.

What's in this book

As the policymakers' definitions of creative industries' center on the generation and commercialization of creativity, ideas, and knowledge, the first chapter explores advertising *creativity*. Even though it does not aim to provide a new definition of creativity, it sheds light on how practitioners comprehend and execute creativity in the sector today. In doing so, the chapter uses creativity as an excuse and a starting point to explore some of the current issues that advertising is demonstrating. The chapter opens by discussing the role of creativity in advertising and highlighting the tensions that can often exist between clients and agencies. These are linked not only to the challenge of bringing creativity to the forefront for clients but also to the sector's struggle to adapt to new business models and monetize creativity in today's media landscape, as the traditional output-based model is no longer viable. The chapter also explores the problems with building new creative cultures that would fit the demand of new generations of talent.

The second chapter discusses *innovation* as another driving force in the advertising industry. It explores how the sector needs to constantly offer new ideas and approaches to keep engaging and persuading consumers, and to rapidly adjust to evolving markets. It also explores how the advertising industry, pushed by the market situation, must expand its scope of services to support its clients and find new revenue sources. At the same time, advertising innovation is not only linked to the capabilities of creative teams. It is also related to agencies' internal cultures and brand attitudes toward creative advertising—their openness to innovative ideas and willingness to take risks. Hence, the chapter also looks into the issues of convincing clients to innovative ideas and creating environments conducive to innovation.

Moving toward analysis of how advertising intersects with other creative sectors, the third chapter explores its relations with audiovisual entertainment. The chapter looks into how advertising and entertainment have started to converge in the early 2000s, with marketers beginning to shift their focus from mass awareness to creating more compelling content that people want to consume. It explores how brands have become storytellers, and why branded entertainment (and brand-sponsored entertainment) has become an important engagement tool. It also investigates why advertisers need to act more like executive producers, and how advertising can learn from Hollywood, not only in terms of storytelling but also in its approach to the creative process.

The fourth chapter further delves into the intersection of advertising and the creative industries. It discusses how brands use arts-centered collaborations as tools for tapping into current social issues and embedding the brand or its message into a (popular) culture. In addition, the chapter considers the complexities that arise in navigating relationships with artists and using intrasectoral collaborations as means for driving in-agency engagement and attracting new talent.

In the concluding chapter, advertising is explored as a regime of paradoxes. As the industry grapples with the tension between established practices and the need for fluidity and constant change, dominant values struggle to maintain their hold. Key tensions include those surrounding creative effectiveness, artistry, collaboration, and the notion of "cool", which speaks to the current state of advertising within the larger realm of the creative industries.

Contextualizing advertising as industrial and cultural

Before exploring the relation between advertising and the creative industries, it is necessary to do some groundwork by considering how creative industries are understood and why advertising's place among them remains in question.

Extensive research and discussion examine the creation of governmental policies and programs to assist the sectors seen as part of the creative industries. There has also been much debate about how cohesive the creative industries are, especially given the dual nature of the processes occurring within creative sectors. For instance, an artist is a cultural producer of works of art, which are objects of exceptional aesthetic and artistic worth. He is also an entrepreneur who invents items that are subsequently sold to customers.[18] As a result, his creations are both a component of a society's culture and a part of its economic system. Such dualism is a feature of the creative economy (and, as follows, the creative industries) that exhibits economic or cultural characteristics depending on the context. It is no different from advertising.

Even though definitions differ slightly from country to country, the creative industries can be understood as a range of economic activities that are concerned with the generation and commercialization of creativity, ideas, knowledge, and information. From the early moments of the paradigm's creation by Australia's government under Paul Keating in the early 1990s,[19] its popularization and ultimate embodiment by the UK's Department of Culture, Media and Sport (DCMS), the tension between the commercial and cultural existed in the discourse about the creative industries. DCMS's inaugural documents tapped into then-buzzy thinking of new economic and technological excitement, the cult of youth, and never-ending organizational upheaval.[20] Even though the "new economy" ultimately lost steam, the concept of creative industries outlasted it and, supported by governmental bodies, found a new life in the 2000s. Promising the new trade potential of "British creativity", DCMS delivered a classification of creative industries that currently lists nine subsectors: (1) advertising and marketing, (2) architecture, (3) crafts, (4) product design, graphics, and fashion design, (5) film, TV, video, radio, and photography, (6) IT, software, and computer services, (7) museums, galleries, and libraries, (8) music, performing, and visual arts, and (9) publishing.[21] These found acceptance as a realistic development model for pushing innovation and monetizing creative powers in numerous countries across the world within only a few years.[22]

While it is evident that the cultural industries preserve *culture* at their core—that is, the anthropological concept that comprises human value systems and institutional frameworks[23]—the work of the creative industries deliberately integrates creativity as a "useful" form of culture into a variety of economic and social policy initiatives. The creative industries framework received mixed reactions as it right away indicated governments' intentions to tie cultural production to a new economic agenda and, therefore, mix arts with politics in what was labeled a "globally contestable policy field".[24] As in the case of Australia's "Creative Nation" policy, designed to assist in embodying new IT prospects and the expanding wave of global culture offered by digital media, the policy was marketed as a cultural strategy although it was mostly an economic agenda.[25] Even though it emphasized culture's importance to national identity and defined culture more broadly than in earlier conceptions by including film, radio, libraries, and other areas, it focused much on the economic potential of cultural activity and arts. It claimed:

> Culture creates wealth. Broadly defined Australian cultural industries generate 13 billion dollars a year. Culture employs . . . Culture adds value; it makes an essential contribution to innovation, marketing and design. The level of creativity substantially determines the ability to adapt to new economic imperatives. It is a valuable export in itself and an essential accompaniment to the export of other commodities. It attracts tourists and students. It is essential to economic success.[26]

Policymakers sought to develop tangible proof that the creative industries are "good for the economy".[27] By including the UK's software sector—the largest single contributor to employment and earnings—among the creative industries, the DCMS was able to increase the sector's employment by 500,000 and income by £36.4 billion in the early 2000s. Hence, while the 1998 *Mapping Documents* assessed the industry's income at £57 billion, the 2001 version increased its value to £112.5 billion, or 5% of GDP.[28] The fact that the creative industries' revenues more than doubled between the 1998 and 2001 editions was attributable, at least in part, to the fact that the two were "not directly comparable", and the different counting methods might explain a large portion of the rise.[29] Similarly, advertising was also coming in handy in boosting the profitability of a young industry even though as a sector itself advertising was reeling from the fallout of the dot.com bubble crash in 2000, which resulted in a drop in shareholder value.[30]

At the same time, the promise of being "good for culture" brought to light the criticism that the creative industries present an overly simplistic narrative linking culture and economy, thereby undermining the argument that culture needs public funding. By extension, the concept has introduced skepticism about the degree to which the creative industries can help resolve the long-standing contradictions between culture and the economy at more conceptual or theoretical levels.[31]

The introduction of the creative industry framework has led to the development of numerous conceptualizations aiming at refining, clarifying, and improving understanding of the creative industries. Many resulted in grouping and modeling sectors into clusters, some building implicit hierarchies, suggesting that some sectors are more at the heart of the industry than others, but each intuitively left advertising at the outer circles of the model. This is exemplified in David Thorsby's "concentric circles model", which locates the creative arts (understood as literature, music, performing arts, and visual arts) at the core, defining them as the "locus of origin of creative ideas".[32] These are followed by cultural industries (heritage services, publishing, and sound), then recording (television, radio, video, and computer games), and finally "related services" (advertising, architecture, design, and fashion) placed at the outer circles. Similarly, in The Work Foundation's proposition, *original* products are put at the heart of the model, followed by cultural industries aimed at *commercialization*, creative industries with their *functional* orientation (such as advertising, design, architecture), and those selling "experiences" (theme parks, museums, and art galleries) at the outermost edge.[33]

The criteria of skills and labor embedded in most of these definitions frame the creative industries as "those industries which have their origin in individual creativity, skill, and talent and which have a potential for wealth and job creation through the generation and exploitation of intellectual property".[34] This has brought additional critique on advertising's place in the circle, with some arguing the need for focusing on the core arts workforce. The issue at hand, they argue, is that the key creative tasks for advertising, such as creative writing and art design, are already covered and classified in other occupations.[35] In their view, copywriting should not be seen as a unique skill on its own but rather belongs to a variety of writing talents, and art design and art direction belong to a broader design category, the same way that designers would be the driving creative force of video gaming. As a result, some would suggest excluding advertising as a substantive sector of the creative industry and connecting it with a dotted line to the applied arts category.

In tandem with the dynamic evolution of creative roles in advertising agencies (or creative agencies, given the ever-broadening scope of their services), it is easy to observe that the sector's traditional key creative stakeholders—copywriters and designers—no longer exhaust the list of creative talent, making the roles hard to categorize within traditional "creative" roles spectrum. Indeed, the DCMS (and similar governmental bodies in other countries) categorizes businesses and professions as creative based on what the organization creates and what individuals perform.[36] This approach causes difficulties that are not immediately apparent. The overall number of creative employees is determined from the sum of all people working in creative sectors, whether or not they are creatively engaged, which means that accountants, security guards, or even cleaners working for a creative agency, record label, concert hall, or theater are considered and counted under the same umbrella of creative staff.[37]

On the other hand, some approaches to characterizing the creative industries seem to romanticize *art for art's sake*,[38] where creators focus on originality, technical professional skills, and the harmony of their creative products and deprioritize profit. They see creators as those who are willing to settle for lower wages than those offered by "humdrum" jobs just to be able to "create".[39] Following this logic, the for-profit orientation of advertising, would disqualify it from being considered a creative industry as its ultimate goal of selling a product or service detracts from the pure artistic expression found in industries such as film, literature, and visual arts. However, conversely, it can be argued that Hollywood's blockbuster-producing machine is more interested in revenues than in artistic and cultural value, given the endless production of sequels, a point that was a key characteristic for Horkheimer and Adorno's classic critique of cultural industries.[40]

Even though bureaucratic cultural policy lies at the heart of the creative industries and lays open to criticism that it is too closely associated with new economy thinking to effectively represent the genuine essence of creativity, the creative industry's core distinction has proven to be robust. This is because it mainstreams the economic worth of culture, media, and design by recognizing that creativity is a key input into modern economies that exhibit culturalization, digitization, and finely designed goods and services.[41]

When we consider advertising as a hybrid form of commercial and cultural production, there emerges an antagonistic tension between promotion and criticality, between its function as a marketing tool and its more diverse potential as a medium for creative experimentation and cultural critique. However, advertising should also be seen as a broader set of cultural practices, going beyond the adaptation of the esthetics of cultural products to being "cultural in various aspects" as expressed by John Sinclair.[42] Advertisements, like other cultural texts, are barometers of societal change. Due to their deep roots in the cultural context, brands such as Nike, Dove, and Ben & Jerry's mirror barely perceptible changes in the values, morality, and behavior of the social groups to whom the message is directed. As advertisers target multiple groups, they frequently wish to mirror their target audiences. In that sense, advertising is a reflection of popular culture, with ads reinforcing trends in fashion, music, and language. Nonetheless, the industry also has an ability to shape popular culture by creating and feeding back into arising trends, oftentimes dictating what is desirable and fashionable, or even socially acceptable. As such, advertising agency employees occupy a unique position as cultural intermediaries.[43] They are responsible not only for creating ad campaigns that appeal to target audiences but also for feeding back to those audiences the trends and influences that they have observed. This way, advertising agencies play a key role in shaping and reflecting the ever-changing face of popular culture operating at the blurred lines between multiple sectors of the industry.

At the same time, as a sector operating within the cultural context, the advertising industry has the capacity to merge goods and services with cultural associations that give them meaning and value beyond their functional benefits. In the mediation of things (as coined by Scott Lash and Celia Lury),[44] advertisers differentiate products one from another, give them memory and personality, and turn them into brands, which allow people to navigate through the complex and oversaturated reality of the consumer goods market. Going further, as brands are not features of products but experiences,[45] advertising creates interfaces of communication between brands and consumers that allow those eventful interactions to happen[46] and give them meanings beyond the basic uses of a product.[47] In effect, whether we like it or not, advertising plays a significant role in fostering consumer literacy in our society.

Notes

1 Krauss, D., & Haggis, P. (Directors). (2018). *5B* [Film]. Hwy61, Saville Productions, f/8 Filmworks.
2 Rooney, D. (2019, May 18). '5B': Film review | Cannes. *The Hollywood Reporter*. https://www.hollywoodreporter.com/movies/movie-reviews/5b-cannes-2019-1212008/.
3 Reddish, D. (2018, November 5). Director Dan Krauss on AIDS doc '5B': "History is, in a very frightening way, repeating itself." *Queerty*. https://www.queerty.com/director-dan-krauss-doc-5b-history-frightening-way-repeating-20181105.
4 O'Barr, W. M. (2011). Creativity in advertising. *Advertising & Society Review*, *11*(4). https://doi.org/10.1353/asr.2011.0006.
5 The shift does not imply that the industry has abandoned push communication, but rather that it is experimenting with new methods of audience engagement in order to provide more genuine value to audiences.
6 Serazio, M. (2013). *Your ad here: The cool sell of guerrilla marketing*. New York University Press.
7 Crawford, M. B. (2016). Introduction, Attention as a cultural problem. In *World beyond your head: On becoming an individual in an age of distraction*. Farrar, Straus & Giroux.
8 Pine, B. J., & Gilmore, J. H. (2020). *The experience economy: Competing for customer time, attention, and money*. Harvard Business Review Press.

9 Kunz, R., Elsässer, F., & Santomier, J. (2016). Sport-related branded entertainment: The Red Bull phenomenon. *Sport, Business and Management: An International Journal, 6*(5). https://doi.org/10.1108/sbm-06-2016-0023.

10 Red Bull Mediahouse. (n.d.). About. *Red Bull Mediahouse.* Retrieved September 8, 2022, from www.redbullmediahouse.com/en/network/red-bull-studios/at.

11 Kunz, R., Elsässer, F., & Santomier, J. (2016). Sport-related branded entertainment: The Red Bull phenomenon. *Sport, Business and Management: An International Journal, 6*(5). https://doi.org/10.1108/sbm-06-2016-0023.

12 Similarly to Serazio's approach to understanding guerilla marketing as "a camouflage on two levels: (1) It shrouds the advertising message in unexpected media spaces, and (2) it also shrouds the fundamental project of consumer management," the forms discussed in this book, that developed from the merging of the commercial and cultural, can be considered as a subtype of guerilla marketing.

13 Even though the trend is commonly considered to be a new approach to think about marketing communication, advertising was already experimenting with blending ads and entertainment decades ago—for example, in brand-sponsored entertainment on American radio in the 1940s and TV in the 1950s.

14 Donaton, S. (2005). *Madison & Vine: Why the entertainment and advertising industries must converge to survive.* McGraw-Hill.

15 Ibid.

16 Although this cultural-advertising product blend cannot, by any stretch of the imagination, be regarded as the most prevalent form of advertising, it must be acknowledged as a distinct category.

17 Havens, T., Lotz, A. D., & Tinic, S. (2009). Critical media industry studies: A research approach. *Communication, Culture & Critique, 2*(2), 234–253. https://doi.org/10.1111/j.1753-9137.2009.01037.x.

18 Louden, S. (2017). *The artist as culture producer: Living and sustaining a creative life.* Intellect.

19 Department of Communications and the Arts (1994, October). Creative nation: Commonwealth cultural policy. https://webarchive.nla.gov.au/awa/20031203235148/http://www.nla.gov.au/creative.nation/contents.html.

20 Lovink, G., & Rossiter, N. (2007). *MyCreativity reader: A critique of creative industries.* Institute of Network Cultures.

21 UK Parliament. (2017). Creative industries sector report. *Parliament.uk.* Retrieved August 23, 2022, from www.parliament.uk/globalassets/documents/commons-committees/Exiting-the-European-Union/17-19/Sectoral-Analyses/10-Creative-Industries-Report.pdf.

22 Ross, A. (2007). Nice work if you can get it: The mercurial career of creative industries policy. In G. Lovink & N. Rossiter (Eds.), *MyCreativity reader: A critique of creative industries* (pp. 17–40). Institute of Network Cultures.

23 Kroeber, A. L., Kluckhohn, C., Meyer, A. G., & Untereiner, W. (1952). *Culture: A critical review of concepts and definitions.* The Museum.

24 Cunningham, S. (2009). Creative industries as a globally contestable policy field. *Chinese Journal of Communication, 2*(1), 13–24. https://doi.org/10.1080/17544750802638814.

25 Moore, I. (2014). Cultural and creative industries concept—a historical perspective. *Procedia—Social and Behavioral Sciences, 110*, 738–746. https://doi.org/10.1016/j.sbspro.2013.12.918.

26 Creative Nation: Commonwealth cultural policy, October 1994, Department of Communications and the Arts (now Office for the Arts), 1994.

27 Banks, M., & O'Connor, J. (2009). After the creative industries. *International Journal of Cultural Policy, 15*(4), 365–373. https://doi.org/10.1080/10286630902989027.

28 Department for Digital, Culture, Media & Sport. (1998, April 9). Creative industries mapping documents 1998. *GOV.UK*. Retrieved September 3, 2022, from www.gov.uk/government/publications/creative-industries-mapping-documents-1998.

29 Heartfield, J. (2005). *The creativity gap*. ETP Ltd.

30 Ibid.

31 Ibid.

32 Throsby, D. (2004). *Economics and culture*. Cambridge University Press.

33 Work Foundation. (2007). *Staying ahead: The economic performance of the UK's creative industries*. Author.

34 Department for Digital, Culture, Media & Sport. (2001, April 9). Creative industries mapping documents 2001. *GOV.UK*. Retrieved September 3, 2022, from www.gov.uk/government/publications/creative-industries-mapping-documents-2001.

35 Wiesand, A., & Söndermann, M. (2005). (rep.). *The "Creative Sector"—an engine for diversity, growth and jobs in Europe. An overview of research findings and debates prepared for the European Cultural Foundation*. European Cultural Foundation.

36 Lovink, G., & Rossiter, N. (2007). *MyCreativity reader: A critique of creative industries*. Institute of Network Cultures.

37 Ibid.

38 Compare: Caves, R. E. (2002). *Creative industries: Contracts between art and commerce*. Harvard University Press.

39 Ibid.

40 Horkheimer, M., & Adorno, T. W. (1972). *Dialectic of enlightenment*. Herder and Herder.

41 Hartley, J., Potts, J., Cunningham, S., Flew, T., Keane, M., & Banks, J. (2013). *Key concepts in creative industries*. SAGE.

42 Sinclair, J. (2018). Advertising as a cultural industry. In K. Oakley & J. O'Connor (Eds.), *The Routledge companion to the cultural industries*. Routledge.

43 Ibid.

44 Lash, S., & Lury, C. (2011). *Global culture industry: The mediation of things*. Polity Press.

45 Ibid.

46 Malik, S. (2005). Information and knowledge. *Theory, Culture & Society*, 29–49. https://doi.org/10.4135/9781446213377.n3.

47 Lash, S., & Urry, J. (2002). *Economies of signs and space*. Sage.

1 Advertising X creativity

"Creativity", says Josh Grossberg, McCann's executive creative director, "by its nature can't have a definition".[1] Oddly enough, as much as creativity is one of the most desirable social competencies, it is also one of the most challenging to pin down.[2] Hence, in today's discourses, not only are people labeled as creative but also processes, spaces, and products.[3] Moreover, the perceptions of creativity vary depending on whom we talk to.[4] Industry judges' views vary from those of customers, students, and industry leaders, and the general public's perceptions change depending on their backgrounds.[5] Even creatives' differences hinge on their function inside an organization.[6] Nonetheless, it appears that scholars have reached some agreement on the concept of creativity in advertising.[7] It is apparent that many academics studying creativity acknowledge that originality, novelty, and newness must be present in at least one aspect of advertising to call it creative.[8] Yet, uniqueness is insufficient,[9] as values of usefulness,[10] problem solving, situational appropriateness, or goal orientation are also necessary features of creative agencies' products.[11]

This approach to creativity seems to be much reflected in practitioners' views as they oftentimes see creativity as a functional tool that helps them to achieve their work goals, more than a personal skill or a value on its own: "creativity is solving a problem . . . in the best way possible",[12] and it is the "art of finding [a] lateral solution to [a] linear problem"[13] or "[creativity is] something that we use to create difference for brands and products and services. We create relevant difference for the clients that we work for".[14]

Even though definitions of creativity, in general, highlight novelty and originality as their universal features,[15] it is worth considering goal orientation as a factor that differentiates creativity in advertising (and, in consequence, possibly differentiates advertising from other creative industries). While sectors derived from the cultural industries might employ creativity to go beyond mastery of crafts or the brilliancy of ideas, in advertising, creativity is always related to an external stakeholder's business aims. Therefore, if we consider it in connection to a client's problem, advertising creativity can be more easily differentiated from entertainment or the arts. Yet, such an approach does not allow for a clear distinction between advertising and creativity applied across

DOI: 10.4324/9781003263128-2

different types of businesses. For example, in the case of software development, the creative process is often driven by user needs and, so, is not only goal oriented but also open-ended: highly affected by processes of interaction between the producers and end-users.[16] It may also happen that user feedback leads to redesigning the product or repurposing its utility. To illustrate, the developers of the popular messaging app WhatsApp probably never envisioned that their product would be used as a tool by Armenian activists to organize the impromptu demonstrations that overthrew the country's dictator,[17] or it would be used to replicate in-person theater experiences during the COVID-19 pandemic.[18] In this sense, it could be argued that creativity in software development is primarily about problem solving. Hence, while recognizing that (business) goal orientation is a helpful differentiating factor, we should also acknowledge the limitations of this approach.

The current discourse on creativity seems to confirm the findings of previous research that advertising creatives' self-definitions focus much on goal-orientation over novelty. The results also showed that participants associated creativity far more with the professional demands and accountabilities of their roles than with personal characteristics or skills. Consequently, we could say that, for advertising professionals, creativity is a means to achieve defined business goals and targets, rather than an end goal. In the business context, due to its intangibility and immeasurability, creativity needs to be seen as a tool of subjective mastery. In dealing with their clients, it is important for agencies to maintain the clients' faith that they can deliver results, making creativity something of a necessarily self-serving ideology. When the client's faith falters, they will go to another agency, a possibility that introduces a constant dimension of instability and risk into the agencies' performance of creativity and, thus, sustains an eternal tension between management and creative staff.

Interestingly, as much as it is commonly accepted that advertising, as an industry, relies heavily on creativity to solve clients' issues and deliver business results, it is common to hear that this reliance on creativity is misguided, and the pursuit of creative ideas and advertising awards sabotages their clients' chances of success.[19] Even though advertising creativity has been shown to have a variety of advantageous effects—a greater desire to review the advertisement,[20] increased attention, depth of processing, and greater recall,[21] as well as favorable influences on ad wear-in,[22] improved brand and ad evaluations,[23] and favorable product evaluations[24]—many believe that ideas that are too far-fetched are less effective at conveying key brand messages. This links to the fact that advertising creativity, as evaluated by a professional (or even by consumers), is not a guarantee of commercial success.[25] For example, Stone, Besser, and Lewis discovered that, while trained judges classified as creative 70% of the advertising that consumers recalled and enjoyed, they also classified as creative 47% of the advertising that audiences strongly disliked.[26] Also, studies show that advertising that is more creative is not better recalled than advertising that is less creative with enough repeated exposure.[27] The benefits of creativity reduce further when the customer pays only partial attention to the marketing communication.[28] This leads (some) marketers to push for repeated ad (over)exposure instead of going through the risk and trouble of approaching advertising efforts creatively. Though this does not allow their brands to stand out in a cluttered market, it might be perceived as a safer option. This is one reason that effectiveness has to be taken more into account in creative advertising. As Dawid Szczepaniak, an executive creative director and partner of VMLY&R, explains:

> One [type of creativity] is of the client's point of view, which is simply looking for new, interesting, fresh ways to solve [the] client's business problems. But it is obvious that *this kind of creativity has nothing to do with the creativity that we associate with creativity festivals.* The second type of creativity is from the point of view of advertising agency employees, so, doing things that are spectacular, absolutely fresh, and unique. Ideally when these two worlds meet, but we all know very well that they meet very rarely.

As expressed in 2008 by Deutsch LA's chief creative officer, Eric Hirshberg, "everything that's wrong with the advertising business can be encapsulated by the fact that we have separated award shows for creativity and effectiveness". Hirshberg compares this to a situation in which the journalism industry would give out one award for writing and another for accuracy.[29] This is something that advertising does on many levels: separating not only creative work and its effects but also considering and celebrating it in terms of various aspects of the craft applied (film, graphic, music, and so on).

The sector's reflection on the topic, and the need for change, can be seen in the increasing prestige of the Effie Awards and the proliferation of new advertising award categories that focus on effectiveness. For instance, in 2011, Lions introduced the Creative Effectiveness Lions, which considers the "impact of creative work" and asks "how an effective strategy rooted in creativity has met its chosen business objectives, how it generated positive customer outcomes and drove sustainable business impact over time".[30] However, this is also not without criticism from inside the industry, with some viewing advertising creativity awards as not much more than the art of writing a strong entry, with bias in favor of large, well-known Western markets. In addition, the discussion of the relationship between advertising creativity and effectiveness extends much further, including the creation of new agency–client partnerships.

From creativity as service to creativity as product

Looking from a legacy perspective, advertising agencies are in the business of selling creativity. In such a model, the client–agency relationship is premised on the delivery of campaign outputs: TV ads, radio spots, posters, advertorials, Internet banners, and many more. In a natural way, the model centers the core *crafts* and artistic skills of advertising: copywriting and art design.[31] An ad's quality can be determined by whether it resonated well with a target audience and drove sales and, from a creative standpoint, whether it was unusual and distinctive.[32] The agency bills the client for creative time spent on conceptualizing and delivering the outputs based on an hourly rate or per delivered output. Hence, we can call this model *creativity-as-service*. While the success of a campaign can certainly impact an agency's bottom line, agencies are ultimately paid for their ideas, not their results. Of course, clients want to see a return on their investments, and an agency's reputation can be damaged by a string of unsuccessful campaigns, but, ultimately, an agency is simply paid to deliver creative work—whether it succeeds or fails. While it is certainly possible for an agency to produce great work without ever seeing any tangible results, it is also true that the best (read: most effective) agencies are often those that are willing to take a chance by trying something new.[33] Nevertheless, this ever-existing model fuels critics who brand advertising creativity as a kind of whim that creatives try to pass off on unsuspecting clients in order to win awards, in what seems to be a never-ending discussion on the value of creativity in advertising.

As the industry evolves, it still holds true that "the craft of advertising is something that . . . makes advertising worth watching",[34] as expressed by Pat Langton, creative director and partner of Melbourne-based Magnum Opus Partners. It can be seen as one of the features that allow for differentiating and recognizing creative advertising.[35] With all-encompassing digitalization, increased consumer ad literacy, emphasis on data and measurement to understand target audiences, always-on culture, and an increasing trend of businesses doing their own advertising "in-house", the role of the creative professionals (so-called creatives) is changing. Where creatives[36] used to be responsible for coming up with big ideas and then executing them flawlessly, now, the emphasis is often on speed and efficiency, and the idea of spending hours honing a single concept seems quaint. While the pace of work and the constant need for delivery of all new content marks the change, there is more to the evolving structure of relationships between agencies and clients.

If, traditionally, agencies were primarily focused on delivering outputs, then, in recent years, with a greater emphasis on ROI and accountability, there has been a move toward understanding success in terms of outcomes. Pierre Odendaal and Steve Clayton, CCO and creative director at McCann Johannesburg, respectively, argue:

Where once advertising creatives would sell their work based on beauty and poetry, we are now measured by our business acumen and strategic prowess. We can no longer sit in the corner daydreaming, while media schedules and demographics are discussed only to stand up with a good looking layout . . . Everything that we do as creative people is still art. The difference is the measure.[37]

This shift is driven by a number of factors, including the increasing transparency of the media landscape and the pressure on marketers to justify their spending. Thus, too, the clients whose roles are focused on delivering against the numbers and specific business goals increasingly transfer this challenge to the creative agencies by attaching tangible and calculable key performance indicators (KPIs) to the creative briefs. Since the digital world enables real-time result tracking and quantification of consumer interest in a campaign, metrics such as engagement rate and conversion have become more important benchmarks of campaign success—and subjects of debate for agencies and clients. As a result, agencies are placing a greater emphasis on understanding the client's business needs and objectives. Hence, goal orientation comes even more to the fore, and the sector is booming with openings for "strategic roles". "Thinkers" are increasingly important stakeholders in the development of creative work. In other words, many agencies look to become providers that can help businesses to achieve success, rather than simply suppliers of deliverables, which calls into question the relationships based purely on deliverables and outputs.

The change calls for a shift in perceptions of how creativity is perceived and operationalized in the agencies' business models and client–agency relationships. Even though advertising agencies have long operated under the principle that creativity is *a service* that they provide to the clients (oriented toward delivering outputs), this model is increasingly giving way to a new understanding of *creativity as a product* (and, as follows, *results as a service*), with creativity being considered a tool for solving client's problems. The change has potentially profound implications for the way agencies do business. As Matt Anderson, CEO and executive creative director of Struck, a Utah-based agency, expresses, "if agencies are honest with themselves—and with their clients—this change is radical".[38] In particular, it means that deliverables and outputs are given lower priority, and scope-of-work agreements are given less consideration. Instead, the focus is on producing creative work that achieves clearly stated goals—a creative brief is unworkable without clearly stated goals, quantifiable KPIs, and an applicable tracking strategy.[39]

Despite many industry professionals supporting the outcomes-as-service model or seeing it as an unavoidable next step for the client–agency relationship, they equally point out that focus on immediate return on investment can come at the expense of long-term brand-building. As a CEO of a New York-based, full-service agency expressed:

> You can push tons of promos sales activations and flash the client results. But it will cost a lot and you will have no brand at the end of the day . . . I think we are forgetting what makes the iconic brands. Like Nike, Nike

as a brand could not have been created overnight and with such approach. And yes, sometimes you have to wait for the effect. Not all can come along with the billing period.

This notion is also shared by some brand representatives, who, despite needing to apply a business-first approach, highlight the necessity of striking the right balance of performance marketing and brand building, and emphasize the importance of timing. Andy Pilkington, the media director for Adidas in Europe, said the following during Campaign Connect:

> The pandemic led to a focus on performance as you can more clearly see a link. You can go to the board and ask for X million Euros and show you'll get X amount back. Whereas it can be much harder to ask for those millions and say what you might gain in brand equity. We've pivoted back now the immediate crisis is over, as if we don't have a strong brand in a few years' time, the performance marketing results won't be sustainable.

Similarly, even though the new model potentially addresses some of the issues in showing the impact of creative work and pushes agencies to consider business efficacy more, it does not come without related problems, starting with defining, strategizing, and measuring advertising effectiveness. The typical models of consumer response to advertising consider the sequence from cognition to affect to behavior.[40] Yet, it has long been proven that advertising does not work by appealing to one's "logical" cognitive processes. Consumer behaviors are, rather, the result of a complex process that begins with perception and ends with memory, which is primarily driven by experiences, emotions, and sentiments (as in a model proposed and tested by Bruce Hall),[41] which relates more to brand building than performance marketing. As such, the idea of consumers' (emotional) engagement potentially becomes another factor differentiating creative advertising (as noncreative works rarely impact engagement), as James Hurman, former Colenso BBDO head of planning, proposes in his book *The Case for Creativity*.[42] In his discussion, Hurman understands engagement as advertising's capacity not only to communicate clearly but also to engage audiences in a way that makes them *voluntarily spend time with the content proposed by a brand*.

The need for developing messages that consumers actually care about (in contrast to those that brands want to tell) becomes clear when we note that consumers, in general, are uninterested in advertising, they would avoid seeing ads if they had a choice, and they are discouraged by the overwhelming amounts of commercial communication encountered every day.[43] Some would go so far as to suggest using voluntary engagement with the content as a metric of success: advertising should be "a communication effort that invites target audiences to watch, engage with or spend time with, out of their own free will or on their own terms".[44] Though this has been an imperative typically for branded entertainment (or brand-sponsored entertainment), some argue that it should be a more common approach to considering advertising success for any brand, as the likeability of content implies, in their view, a positive outcome on the brand perception. This notion will be discussed more in Chapter 3.

"Owning" the client

Throughout the 20th century, media buying was a marginalized and subservient function. This began to shift during the 1960s when big advertising firms created specialized media buy departments. By the 1980s and 1990s, several global media companies had branched out and established themselves as a major industry in their own right.[45] Media agencies developed alongside the digital advertising market since the late 1990s. As performance trackers and measurements grow in importance, the advertising industry's center of gravity has shifted, giving media planning and buying excessive weight within the links between brands, agencies, and publishers.[46] Since platforms have become increasingly important channels for content consumption, media agencies act as a link between platforms and content producers, enhancing the platform mechanisms of datafication, commodification, and selection. In so doing, media agencies contribute to the platformization of the news media and other sectors. While they might not understand themselves as cultural intermediaries, they are indeed producing symbolic value[47] and mediating between culture and economy, and culture and consumption,[48] which is not without consequences for their position in the media landscape. By advising advertisers on where and how to spend their budgets, media agencies have become crucial players in the media business, impacting media markets and the digital media infrastructure[49] and finding themselves not only in the business of media planning and buying but also becoming a driving force and a controller of media ecosystems having the access to and say about the vast commercial budget.

However, media agencies' position has also evolved dramatically during the last decade in relation to their clients—from offering space in paid traditional and electronic media to advising marketers on broader marketing strategies and media purchases, and enabling them across all kinds of paid, owned, earned, and shared media.[50] Therefore, by controlling budgets and offering an increasingly broad range of services, media agencies have become key advisors. As the chief operating officer of a Europe-based network media agency explained,

> We no longer believe we should limit ourselves to media planning and buying. We perform a variety of strategic and advisory services for our clients. And it's something we're already . . . quite used to—access to data

has enabled us to finally get a handle on the audiences, so now it comes as second nature.

In their mission to offer comprehensive services to marketers, media agencies increasingly become media conglomerates for a full range of services. This trend has a direct impact on creative agencies that are seeing their businesses undermined by the expanding operations of their competitors. It is particularly important to acknowledge that media agencies began to encroach on the territories traditionally reserved for advertising agencies (among others). As Josh Grossberg expressed:

> It's all about who controls the money in a weird way . . . Media has won the whole battle. Like, I think I would not be surprised if not before long media companies will own the creative as well, because you spend a million dollars making a TV commercial, that's a rounding error on your broadcast budget. Awesome, right? Let's throw that in [for a client] for free.

As media agencies increasingly develop specialized services, they move into the area of content production and, therefore, are also becoming more formidable rivals for ad money. Even though they may not see themselves as media or content producers,[51] but—as Napoli and Caplan claimed—that they are.[52] At the same time, they operate on a different business model with extensively higher budgets than creative agencies, potentially meaning that they can expand their scope of services to offer creative work in packages along with media planning and buying, thereby keeping all the clients' business under their roof. They can even add output production free of charge to the executed campaigns, as Grossberg indicates.

However, not only media agencies undermine the business of creative agencies; the lines between advertising, media, marketing, and PR are increasingly blurred with no clear distinction of responsibilities between various kinds of agencies. This makes the marketplace increasingly difficult for creative agencies. Some industry insiders link this to the fragmentation of the media market and target audiences since there are countless ways and platforms for consumers to access media in today's media ecosystem. It is, therefore, not surprising (even though many creatives critique the approach as "a waste of time and effort") that advertisers "shop around", using the services of multiple kinds of specialized entities, rather than spending the majority of their budgets on one kind of activity (as they used to in the golden era of TVCs). Media agencies often function as a glue for all brand activities and, thereby, take precedence in leading clients' thinking and choices. As Grossberg continues:

> Maybe it's just about targeting now and less about messaging. If I could fix one thing about the advertising industry, I would say it is that we as

advertisers have given away what it is that we sell, and we've devalued it. I think what we sell is, yes, smart targeting. And yes, it's smart strategy. But really what we sell is communications that speak to people and motivate them. And a lot of times I think we have given that away, and we don't defend what that is, and the value of it highly enough.

Creative agencies are, therefore, under increasing pressure to adapt and provide more comprehensive service, often working on brand work or even product development. For some creatives, this entails exciting new chances to use their creativity in novel contexts, but it may also lead to internal and client—agency conflicts, necessitating the establishment of a more innovative workplace environment.

This transformation is upsetting to many leaders, as they believe that it has upended the status quo with regard to who holds exclusive ownership over creative work commissioned by clients. The "old system", in which a single creative team was responsible for all aspects of a campaign from strategy to execution, is no longer the norm. Instead, campaigns are often divided among multiple agencies, each with its own specialized focus. This fragmentation has led to greater competition among creatives and has made it more difficult for any one team to lay claim to the entire creative vision for a given project. While some see this as a positive development that encourages collaborative effort with more diverse voices and perspectives (discussed further in Chapter 3), others, like Grossberg, worry about their position in the ecosystem:

> I think that we as an agency world have given away that sort of moral high ground about what it is that we produce. Like, once upon a time, you would go to an agency because of who the creatives and account people were, because of who the personalities were. And I think we've sort of erased that, and I think that valuing what we do, the ability to see a client's business and see what story it is, that we are, how we want people to relate to us to that client. That's what we've sort of thrown out a little bit or devalued.[53]

Creating within the market's complexity

In a competitive market with numerous industry organizations supplying overlapping services and vying for limited client money, creative agencies must now also compete with brand clients who are increasingly bringing marketing activities in-house and consultants encroaching on their domain. Agencies must necessarily look for new revenue streams and create more value for their clients in order to make a return on their investments. In turn, it is not uncommon to see that business models and product innovations are co-created together by a brand and an agency. In such cases, the agency is effectively acting as a research, development, or business consultant for the client. This is a far cry from the traditional role of the agency as a provider of media space and creative brand messaging. If we consider the scope of services of creative agencies today, we see that advertising bodies now position themselves as more well-rounded business advisors, competing for clients not only with other creative agencies but also with consulting agencies. "Agencies have to step into a different model, which is about marketing, consulting, and making sure that they understand data management and orchestrating platforms", argues Bob Ray, worldwide CEO of DWA, which is owned by Merkle.[54] Even though agencies and their parent companies are rapidly expanding their strategic business services and technology integration capabilities, the road is steep, and the economics are difficult.

With investment going toward both gearing up agencies with consultancy expertise and the other way around—consulting corporations building creative structures—the true distinction for a brand marketer may be less about talent and more about business connections. High-profile acquisitions by both sides at the beginning of the 2020s highlight the rush to shift perception and attain parity in these crucial competencies. Accenture's 2019 acquisition of famed independent agency Droga5[55] on the consulting side of the ledger, for example, challenges the notion that consultancies cannot provide a platform for creativity. Both organizations are as cautious to highlight cultural fit and creative capabilities as they are to make the argument for commercial competitiveness.

Critiques of these mergers express not only a lack of cultural fit but also point out that many joint agencies started as design firms or formed through mergers between consultancies and designers. As a result, pessimists suggest that these agencies frequently change the visual identity of their clients' brands, owing to the agencies' prior experience in design, rather than delivering highly relevant consumer experiences that have a truly meaningful business impact.

The growing convergence between the consultancy and agency worlds does not necessarily go smoothly on the agency side either. As advertising agencies need to compete in an increasingly complex advertising ecosystem, the intricacy of advertising-related jobs and businesses generates tension related to what the industry is today and the scope of the services that are offered. As Josh Grossberg expressed:

> I think it [the lack of clear identity of advertising agencies] is led, in a weird way, to a lack of focus on what it is what we do. But at the same way, it's like kind of healthier as a creative because I get to play with everything. All these things that used to get me thrown out of the room before, you know.

Or, as Nicoletta Stefanidou, a co-founder and CCO at Tinker Tailor, said, "It's about the brand today. We need to communicate the brand. It doesn't always pan out to be advertising. . . . It could be a new product; it could be anything. It's still creative work". Even though the work in advertising has always required massive flexibility and the ability to learn quickly,[56] the complexity that now comes standard with advertising, design, consulting, and digital services leads sometimes to uncertainty. Although the varied tasks are exciting, some creatives feel they could be handled better elsewhere: "As a creative director, I want to own a lot of things, that, probably, I shouldn't. Like, I feel like 'okay, I've got enough of the background to do things that I maybe wouldn't have in the past. But there are times when I should very well give it over to somebody else'" as Grossberg continues his divagations.

Creatives appear to have "a love–hate relationship" with the constraints imposed by strategic considerations on advertising.[57] Previous research shows that creatives value clients who give them the freedom to experiment with new ideas, but they also thought there was an inadequate challenge until their work was driven by a rigid strategy.[58] Despite the fact that comprehensive services, more consulting work, and business-oriented, numbers-driven tasks should be beneficial in terms of defining boundaries and giving direction, it also brings struggles related to the creative process. In the current culture, where creatives are expected to innovate constantly, tasks that focus on open-ended projects may be more challenging for agencies to plan[59] compared to tasks with specific, preagreed deliverables.[60] When the output is unspecified, it might range from developing a new product to inventing a unique way of communicating or coming up with a new platform for message delivery. Under such conditions, creative directors have trouble determining what talents and resources will be required to bring their project to completion. At the same time, creatives must keep themselves engaged in a fast-paced, demanding setting.[61] They do this by adapting their engagements to their customers' changing demands (a process referred to as morphing by Laurey, Berends, and Huysman)[62] while allowing their clients to participate in creative work on their own (mobilization).[63] As a result, clients get what they want, but the nature of the innovative undertaking has changed—each project in advertising lays the foundation for future projects and opens new paths for further consideration.[64]

Creativity without creative talent

"If we don't continue to prove that creativity directly affects the bottom line of business, we won't get the investment. If we don't get the investment, then we won't pull in the talent. If we don't pull in the talent then it's a slippery slope to where the industry will, I think, need a lot of help", says Susan Credle, the global chief creative officer at FCB Global, cited in the Cannes Lions' Creativity Report. She links the business aspects of a changing advertising environment with the industry's increasing issue of attracting and retaining creative staff.

More than a tool of the advertising industry, creativity needs to be understood as a feature of a creative person, "who regularly solves problems, fashions products, or defines new questions in a domain in a way that is initially considered novel but that ultimately becomes accepted in a particular cultural setting", according to Gardner.[65] As Mihaly Csikszentmihalyi conceptualized, "creativity results from the interaction of a system composed of three elements: a culture that contains symbolic rules, a person who brings novelty into the symbolic domain, and a field of experts who recognize and validate the innovation".[66] Creative agencies are complex social settings that make space for creativity to thrive, but they are also people-driven businesses. They require a steady supply of a very specific kind of staff (creatives) with expansive tendencies—ready to explore, seek novelty, take risks,[67] and prepared to take on the ever-changing tasks and functions required to operate in dynamic environments. To offer their customers challenging, innovative thinking that propels their brands and companies ahead, advertising creatives need to continually deliver infusions of fresh ideas.

The postpandemic "great resignation" that affected many sectors, with workers reevaluating their priorities and expectations, only exacerbated an already bleak talent retention situation. Speaking to agency leaders about what their company's most pressing issues are, the problem of attracting and retaining new talent comes up time and time again. Also, according to research with more than 700 marketing professionals conducted by Hays recruiting agency and the Chartered Institute of Marketing, more than 60% of marketers planned to change jobs in 2021. According to their report, career expectations have changed dramatically since the COVID-19 pandemic began. Employees desire greater work–life balance that enhances their independence.[68]

The problem is not simply about monetary investment, as mentioned by Credle, or work–life balance, and commute-free hybrid workplaces. The advertising industry, which took pride in being forward-thinking and adaptable and offering a stimulating working environment, compared to other industries, no longer appears as appealing to many people. As Nixon and Crewe pointed out already in 2004, the freedom, informality, and glamour of work in advertising are exaggerated.[69] Rather, it is characterized through the lens of hierarchical office structures, high pressure, long working hours, and limited creative control. Also, the social meaning of being an industry associated with coolness, machoism, and workaholism no longer resonates with younger generations.[70] As one US-based senior executive explained:

> Twenty years ago, every art school or art college kid wanted to work in ads. Working in ads meant something and meant big. You could even say that it had its snobbish prestige. Now? They can more clearly see that our industry is not all glitter and champagne, and the culture in ads can be toxic. And they just don't want to be part of that. Long working hours that we used to see as dedication to our jobs, they see as no personal life. And

they want to have life, even if they make less, which was unbelievably rare to see few years back.

High pressure and the expectation of on-demand creativity contribute to burn-out among the sector's employees. The (perceived) lack of job security in advertising and the frequent presence of agency politics reduce the internal drive required for creative work. Increasingly, talent seeks jobs that fit better with their personal values. Twenty-two per cent of the sector's employees want to seek a new professional path in search of a "higher purpose".[71] This also holds true for many young people entering the job market. As Nikhil Narayanan, former creative director at Ogilvy India, now at Tata Consultancy Services, explains:

> We were loyal to work, bosses, career, etc. As a result, we normalized and surrendered to toxicity in the industry. The younger generation is loyal to their mental health, organizational ethics, employer purpose, authenticity, work—life balance, etc.—something that ad agencies are struggling to provide. They are, in fact, fighting the toxicity we inadvertently endorsed. It isn't that the younger generation is disloyal. They are just loyal to different things.

Or, as a London-based executive creative director expressed, "with pressing issues like climate issues, pandemic, war conflicts and brands greenwashing, creating emotional bonds between consumers and snack brand does not seem to be pressing enough to care about". Many young creatives look to start-ups, which offer potentially lower pay and longer hours, but come with the promise of growing with the business and seeing the impact of their work. Alternatively, because contract work is thriving again, many are leaving staff jobs for freelance. In fact, an estimated 50% of the ad industry could be freelance within the next decade.[72] Others become, as James Cooper labels them, "armchair entrepreneurs", who dream of leaving but are not ready to give up on the steady paycheck, security, and related lifestyle.[73]

The fact that advertising agencies have a problem with attracting and retaining talent leads to several consequences, both for the agencies themselves and for their relationships with clients. "Both internally and client-side, agencies are facing the challenges that come with having new team members, loss of legacy knowledge, and shifts in work methodologies", says Loren Blandon, global head of learning, growth, and experiences at VMLY&R. As experienced employees leave and are not easily replaced, the average level of experience and expertise within the agency is at risk of decreasing, which is also visible to clients. As Jessica Spence, president of brands at Beam Suntory, explained in the documentary *Kill your darlings*, which explores an issue of talent detachment:

> I think historically, the view was the big agency networks, that was their guarantee [that they have top talent and a pipeline to make sure they offer

them to their clients]. And I don't think that's true anymore ... And I think that's because the industry went down a path of thinking it was something you could scale ... They are no longer magnets for talent.

Notes

1 J. Grossberg, personal communication, April 20, 2022.
2 Goldenberg, J., Levav, A., Mazursky, D., & Solomon, S. (2009). *Cracking the ad code*. Cambridge University Press.
3 Sternberg, R. J., & Lubart, T. I. (2009). The concept of creativity: Prospects and paradigms. In R. J. Sternberg (Ed.), *Handbook of creativity* (pp. 3–15). Cambridge University Press; Edward, N. (2011). *Psychologia twórczości*. Gdańskie Wydawnictwo Psychologiczne.
4 Koslow, S., Sasser, S. L., & Riordan, E. A. (2003). What is creative to whom and why? *Journal of Advertising Research*, *43*(1), 96–110. https://doi.org/10.2501/jar-43-1-96-110.
5 White, A., & Smith, B. L. (2001). Assessing advertising creativity using the creative product semantic scale. *Journal of Advertising Research*, *41*(6), 27–34. https://doi.org/10.2501/jar-41-6-27-34.
6 Hirschman, E. C. (1989). Role-based models of advertising creation and production. *Journal of Advertising*, *18*(4), 42–53. https://doi.org/10.1080/00913367.1989.10673166.
7 Koslow, S., Sasser, S. L., & Riordan, E. A. (2003). What is creative to whom and why? *Journal of Advertising Research*, *43*(1), 96–110. https://doi.org/10.2501/jar-43-1-96-110.
8 Sternberg, R. J., & Lubart, T. I. (1996). Investing in creativity. *American Psychologist*, *51*(7), 677–688. https://doi.org/10.1037/0003-066x.51.7.677.
9 Mumford, M. D., & Gustafson, S. B. (1988). Creativity syndrome: Integration, application, and innovation. *Psychological Bulletin*, *103*(1), 27–43. https://doi.org/10.1037/0033-2909.103.1.27.
10 Rothenberg, A., & Hausman, C. R. (1976). *The creativity question*. Duke University Press.
11 MacKinnon, D. W. (1965). Personality and the realization of creative potential. *American Psychologist*, *20*(4), 273–281. https://doi.org/10.1037/h0022403; Following O'Quin & Besemer's writing, *creative products* should be understood in a liberal and inclusive sense to refer to both ideas and observable outcomes. (O'Quin, K., & Besemer, S. P. (2020). Creative products. In M. A. Runco & S. R. Pritzker (Eds.), *Encyclopedia of creativity* (pp. 413–422). Academic Press.)
12 L. Enebeis, personal communication, January 5, 2022.
13 Odendaal, P., & Clayton, S. (2014). Creativity: From art to intelligence. In D. Fiandaca, A. Andjelic, & G. Kay (Eds.), *Hacker, maker, teacher, thief: Advertising's next generation*. Creative Social.
14 B. Korsten, personal communication, February 24, 2022.
15 Amabile, T. M. (1996). *Creativity in context: Update to the social psychology of creativity*. Routledge; Boden, M. A. (1990). *The creative mind: Myths & mechanisms*. Weidenfield and Nicolson; Leadbeater, C. (1999). *Living on thin air: The new economy*. Viking; Mockros, C., & Csikszentmihalyi, M. (1999). Part four: creativity at work. The social construction of creative lives. In A. Montuori & R. E. Purser (Eds.), *Social creativity*. Hampton Press.
16 Steiner, M., & Prettenthaler, F. (2015). Creativity reconsidered—so your firm is creative, but how much? A trans-sectoral and continuous approach to creative industries. *Regional Studies, Regional Science*, *2*(1), 275–289. https://doi.org/10.1080/21681376.2015.1016097.

17 Clarke, K., & Koçak, K. (2021, December 7). Eight years after Egypt's revolution, here's what we've learned about social media and protest. *The Washington Post*. Retrieved September 4, 2022, from www.washingtonpost.com/news/monkey-cage/wp/2019/01/25/eight-years-after-egypts-revolution-heres-what-weve-learned-about-social-media-and-protest/.

18 Goldmann, A. J. (2021, February 11). Theaters go digital to talk about life (and death) in the pandemic. *The New York Times*. Retrieved September 4, 2022, from www.nytimes.com/2021/02/11/theater/werther-live-sterberaum.html.

19 Compare: Hurman, J. (2016). *The case for creativity: The link between imaginative marketing & commercial success*. Cannes Lions.

20 Yang, X., & Smith, R. E. (2009). Beyond attention effects: Modeling the persuasive and emotional effects of advertising creativity. *Marketing Science, 28*(5), 935–949. https://doi.org/10.1287/mksc.1080.0460.

21 Jin, H. S., Kerr, G., Suh, J., Kim, H. J., & Sheehan, B. (2022). The power of creative advertising: Creative ads impair recall and attitudes toward other ads. *International Journal of Advertising, 41*, 1521–1540. https://doi.org/10.1080/02650487.2022.2045817; Lehnert, K., Till, B. D., & Carlson, B. D. (2013). Advertising creativity and repetition. *International Journal of Advertising, 32*(2), 211–231. https://doi.org/10.2501/ija-32-2-211-231; Sheinin, D. A., Varki, S., & Ashley, C. (2011). The differential effect of ad novelty and message usefulness on brand judgments. *Journal of Advertising, 40*(3), 5–18. https://doi.org/10.2753/joa0091-3367400301; Smith, R. E., Chen, J., & Yang, X. (2008). The impact of advertising creativity on the hierarchy of effects. *Journal of Advertising, 37*(4), 47–62. https://doi.org/10.2753/joa0091-3367370404; Yang, X., & Smith, R. E. (2009). Beyond attention effects: Modeling the persuasive and emotional effects of advertising creativity. *Marketing Science, 28*(5), 935–949. https://doi.org/10.1287/mksc.1080.0460.

22 Chen, J., Yang, X., & Smith, R. E. (2014). The effects of creativity on advertising wear-in and wear-out. *Journal of the Academy of Marketing Science, 44*(3), 334–349. https://doi.org/10.1007/s11747-014-0414-5.

23 Ang, S. H., & Low, S. Y. (2000). Exploring the dimensions of ad creativity. *Psychology & Marketing, 17*(10), 835–854. https://doi.org/10.1002/1520-6793(200010)17:10; Till, B. D., & Baack, D. W. (2005). Recall and persuasion: Does creative advertising matter? *Journal of Advertising, 34*(3), 47–57. https://doi.org/10.1080/00913367.2005.10639201.

24 Dahlen, M., Rosengren, S., & Karsberg, J. (2018). The effects of signaling monetary and creative effort in ads. *Journal of Advertising Research, 58*(4), 433–442. https://doi.org/10.2501/jar-2018-013; Dahlén, M., & Lange, F. (2005). Advertising weak and strong brands: Who gains? *Psychology & Marketing, 22*(6), 473–488. https://doi.org/10.1002/mar.20069.

25 Kover, A. J., James, W., & Sonner, B. S. (1997). To whom do advertising creatives write? An inferential answer. *Journal of Advertising Research, 37*(1); Vaughan, K., Beal, V., & Romaniuk, J. (2016). Can brand users really remember advertising more than nonusers? Testing an empirical generalization across six advertising awareness measures. *Journal of Advertising Research, 56*(3). https://doi.org/10.2501/jar-2016-037; West, D., Koslow, S., & Kilgour, M. (2019). Future directions for advertising creativity research. *Journal of Advertising, 48*(1), 102–114. https://doi.org/10.1080/00913367.2019.1585307.

26 Stone, G., Besser, D., & Lewis, L. E. (2000). Recall, liking, and creativity in TV commercials: A new approach. *Journal of Advertising Research, 40*(3), 7–18. https://doi.org/10.2501/jar-40-3-7-18.

27 Chen, J., Yang, X., & Smith, R. E. (2014). The effects of creativity on advertising wear-in and wear-out. *Journal of the Academy of Marketing Science, 44*(3), 334–349. https://doi.org/10.1007/s11747-014-0414-5; Lehnert, K., Till, B. D., &

Carlson, B. D. (2013). Advertising creativity and repetition. *International Journal of Advertising*, *32*(2), 211–231. https://doi.org/10.2501/ija-32-2-211-231.

28 Baack, D. W., Wilson, R. T., & Till, B. D. (2008). Creativity and memory effects: Recall, recognition, and an exploration of nontraditional media. *Journal of Advertising*, *37*(4), 85–94. https://doi.org/10.2753/joa0091-3367370407.

29 Hirshberg, E. (2008, August 25). Commercial art must be both. *Ad Age*. Retrieved September 4, 2022, from https://adage.com/article/awards-08/commercial-art/130130.

30 Cannes Lions. (2022). *Creative effectiveness lions*. Cannes Lions.

31 Shore, T. W. (1907). The craft of the advertiser. *Fortnightly Review*, May 1865–June 1934, *81*(482).

32 Robinson, T. (2019, June 3). Why craft matters in advertising. *Creative Review*. Retrieved September 7, 2022, from www.creativereview.co.uk/why-craft-matters-in-advertising.

33 Hurman, J. (2016). *The case for creativity: The link between imaginative marketing & commercial success*. Cannes Lions.

34 Langton, P. (2018, April 30). Is craft dead in advertising? *Campaign Brief*. Retrieved September 7, 2022, from https://campaignbrief.com/pat-langton-is-craft-dead-in-a/.

35 Hurman, J. (2016). *The case for creativity: The link between imaginative marketing & commercial success*. Cannes Lions.

36 In advertising, creative professionals are informally known as "creatives." This encompasses copywriters, art directors, creative directors, and broadcast producers—the traditional roles considered to be on the creative side of advertising (Moriarty & Vandenbergh, 1984). However, as the market evolves, an increasing number of roles can be considered "creative." E.g., people who specialize in developing ad campaigns or those who focus on digital marketing may also be considered creatives. (Moriarty, S. E., & Vandenbergh, B. G. (1984). Advertising creatives look at creativity. *The Journal of Creative Behavior*, *18*(3), 162–174. https://doi.org/10.1002/j.2162-6057.1984.tb00380.x).

37 Odendaal, P., & Clayton, S. (2014). Creativity: From art to intelligence. In D. Fiandaca, A. Andjelic, & G. Kay (Eds.), *Hacker, maker, teacher, thief: Advertising's next generation*. Creative Social.

38 Andreson, M. (2016, October 11). The end of 'creativity as a service'. *Medium. com*. Retrieved September 7, 2022, from https://medium.com/experienceaffinity/the-end-of-creativity-as-a-service-2a8e6ba2d825.

39 Ibid.

40 Hall, B. F. (2002). A new model for measuring advertising effectiveness. *Journal of Advertising Research*, *42*(2), 23–31. https://doi.org/10.2501/jar-42-2-23-31.

41 Ibid.

42 Hurman, J. (2016). *The case for creativity: The link between imaginative marketing & commercial success*. Cannes Lions.

43 Dahlén, M., Rosengren, S., & Törn, F. (2008). Advertising creativity matters. *Journal of Advertising Research*, *48*(3), 392–403. https://doi.org/10.2501/s002184990808046x.

44 van Loggerenberg, M. J. C., Enslin, C., & Terblanche-Smit, M. (2019). Towards a definition for branded entertainment: An exploratory study. *Journal of Marketing Communications*, *27*(3), 322–342. https://doi.org/10.1080/13527266.2019.1643395.

45 Pratt, A. C. (2006). Advertising and creativity, a governance approach: A case study of creative agencies in London. *Environment and Planning A: Economy and Space*, *38*(10), 1883–1899. https://doi.org/10.1068/a38261.

46 Turow, J. (2011). *The daily you*. Yale University Press.

47 Maguire, J. S., & Matthews, J. (2012). Are we all cultural intermediaries now? An introduction to cultural intermediaries in context. *European Journal of Cultural Studies*, *15*(5), 551–562. https://doi.org/10.1177/1367549412445762.

48 Cronin, A. M. (2004). Regimes of mediation: Advertising practitioners as cultural intermediaries? *Consumption Markets & Culture*, 7(4), 349–369. https://doi.org/10.1080/1025386042000316315.

49 Willig, I. (2021). From audiences to data points: The role of media agencies in the platformization of the news media industry. *Media, Culture & Society*, 44(1), 56–71. https://doi.org/10.1177/01634437211029861.

50 Jensen, H., & Sund, K. J. (2017). The journey of business model innovation in media agencies: Towards a three-stage process model. *Journal of Media Business Studies*, 14(4), 282–298. https://doi.org/10.1080/16522354.2018.1445158.

51 Willig, I. (2021). From audiences to data points: The role of media agencies in the platformization of the news media industry. *Media, Culture & Society*, 44(1), 56–71. https://doi.org/10.1177/01634437211029861.

52 Napoli, P., & Caplan, R. (2017). Why media companies insist they're not media companies, why they're wrong, and why it matters. *First Monday*, 22(5). https://doi.org/10.5210/fm.v22i5.7051.

53 J. Grossberg, personal communication, April 20, 2022.

54 Benes, R. (2019, May 6). How are ad agencies competing with consultancies? *Insider Intelligence*. Retrieved October 16, 2022, from www.insiderintelligence.com/content/to-stay-competitive-ad-agencies-mimic-consultancies.

55 Accenture. (2019). Accenture interactive completes acquisition of Creative Agency, DROGA5. *Newsroom*. Retrieved October 16, 2022, from https://newsroom.accenture.com/news/accenture-interactive-completes-acquisition-of-creative-agency-droga5.htm.

56 Barone, M. J., & Jewell, R. D. (2013). How brand innovativeness creates advertising flexibility. *Journal of the Academy of Marketing Science*, 42(3), 309–321. https://doi.org/10.1007/s11747-013-0352-7.

57 Koslow, S., Sasser, S. L., & Riordan, E. A. (2003). What is creative to whom and why? *Journal of Advertising Research*, 43(1), 96–110. https://doi.org/10.2501/jar-43-1-96-110.

58 Ibid.

59 Laurey, N., Berends, H., & Huysman, M. (2017). Creativity as a service: How creative agents foster a liminal experience. *Academy of Management Proceedings*, 2017(1), 15620. https://doi.org/10.5465/ambpp.2017.261.

60 Ibid.

61 Cohendet, P., Lleren, P., & Simon, L. (2014). The routinization of creativity. *Frontiers in Evolutionary Economics*, 120–141. https://doi.org/10.1515/9783110509205-002; Patriotta, G., & Hirsch, P. M. (2016). Mainstreaming innovation in art worlds: Cooperative links, conventions and amphibious artists. *Organization Studies*, 37(6), 867–887. https://doi.org/10.1177/0170840615622062.

62 Laurey, N., Berends, H., & Huysman, M. (2017). Creativity as a service: How creative agents foster a liminal experience. *Academy of Management Proceedings*, 2017(1), 15620. https://doi.org/10.5465/ambpp.2017.261.

63 Ibid.

64 Ibid.

65 Gardner, H. E. (2011). *Creating minds*. Basic Books.

66 Csikszentmihalyi, M. (1997). *Creativity: Flow & the psychology of discovery & invention*. Harper & Row.

67 Ibid.

68 Jefferson, M. (2021, May 18). Two-thirds of marketing employers plan to hire this year as Covid tails off. *Marketing Week*. Retrieved September 7, 2022, from www.marketingweek.com/marketing-employers-hire/.

69 Nixon, S., & Crewe, B. (2004). Pleasure at work? Gender, consumption and work-based identities in the creative industries. *Consumption Markets & Culture*, 7(2), 129–147. https://doi.org/10.1080/1025386042000246197.

70 Ibid.
71 Jefferson, M. (2021, May 18). Two-thirds of marketing employers plan to hire this year as Covid tails off. *Marketing Week*. Retrieved September 7, 2022, from www.marketingweek.com/marketing-employers-hire/.
72 Berlin, E. (2022, January 31). How the great resignation is impacting the ad industry. *Ad Age*. Retrieved September 7, 2022, from https://adage.com/article/best-places-work/how-great-resignation-impacting-ad-industry/2392011.
73 Cooper, J. (2014). Skin in the game: The curious phenomenon of agencies and start-ups. In D. Fiandaca, A. Andjelic, & G. Kay (Eds.), *Hacker, maker, teacher, thief: Advertising's next generation* (pp. 187–198). Creative Social.

2   Advertising X innovation

ING is a Dutch banking company, involved for over a dozen years in sponsoring arts and culture in the Netherlands and worldwide. One of the entities that it sponsors is the Rijksmuseum in Amsterdam, a pearl in the Dutch art sector crown. The museum is known for holding Dutch art from the Middle Ages to the 20th century, including masterpieces by Rembrandt and Vermeer. It has a reputation for being traditional rather than modern, with a focus on the Old Masters and Dutch ancestry. As 2015 was about to mark ten years of partnership between ING and Rijksmuseum, the brand turned to their creative agency, JWT (now Wunderman Thompson), to help them come up with an idea that would celebrate their relationship with arts and culture with an innovative spin—as innovation lay at the core of ING's brand positioning. "It was in the time where people were looking at AI [artificial intelligence]. And we were sometimes also scared of where AI could go. But at that point in time, it didn't really go into the creative world just yet", Bas Korsten, the agency's chief creative officer explains. This was the origin of the idea to bring Rembrandt, one of the Dutch Masters, to life to produce yet another masterpiece 347 years after his death. Only this time, the painter was data, and the brush was technology.

The Next Rembrandt campaign was based on the idea of creating an all-new, 3D-printed painting "by Rembrandt" created entirely from the data collected in the processes of analyzing Rembrandt's existing works. The creative team began their design efforts by compiling a full collection of paintings, creating high-resolution scans of all 346 Rembrandt works. Then, the time came for the first key creative choice: deciding the subject of a new 3D portrait. The agency analyzed the subjects of all Rembrandt's paintings, over 400 faces, and concluded that the new sitter should be roughly 30 to 40 years old, male, wearing black clothing, a hat, and facing the right. From the angle of relevance and recurrence, more than 6,000 face landmarks were employed to categorize the traits of his subjects. Based on these characteristics, the computer learned how to build a typical face for Rembrandt's style and, following the creation of the various features, integrated them into a completely formed face and chest in the manner of Rembrandt's proportions. The team added another dimension to go from a 2D graphic to a 3D-printed artwork.

DOI: 10.4324/9781003263128-3

They accomplished this by mixing three layers: canvas, ground layer, and brushstrokes. Brushstrokes were created by employing X-ray images of Rembrandt's original pieces to educate the system and match similar geometric motifs between the source paintings and the new portrait. The painting was then printed with a custom-built 3D printer that was specifically designed to reproduce existing artwork but had never been utilized to make a new artwork before. To bring The Next Rembrandt to life, the machine printed 13 layers of paint-based UV ink. The process took 18 months and a team of 20 data analysts, scientists, developers, and 3D printing experts, not including the creative team behind the idea.[1]

Figure 2.1 Next Rembrandt

Source: Wunderman Thompson Amsterdam

In the case of Next Rembrandt, the brand's objective was to link a desire to be seen as modern and innovative with its patronage of art and culture of a rather traditional character. To do so, the agency developed a plan that utilized data, new technologies, and communication channels while also forming numerous partnerships (such as with Microsoft, Canon, Mauritshuis Museum, and the Delft University of Technology) to create cutting-edge content and expose the company's values. The JWT team also acknowledged the importance of their campaign's timing. While there was debate about whether machines will ever be able to take over creative duties and render copywriters and art directors obsolete, the firm has brought AI technology into the human toolbox as a source of inspiration and fuel. However, the case's inventiveness went further, as it blurred the boundaries between data, technology, and art by providing (together with the research institutions involved in the project) a tool of more practical applicability. The technology developed for The Next Rembrandt is now being used to restore damaged and partially lost masterpieces, and parts of the solution's code have been made open source to aid future advancements, thus transcending the campaign's boundaries and fueling other sectors with innovative solutions. Recalling that time, Bas Korsten explains:

> We're in the business of making a difference. Sometimes that difference is in the way that we tell a story. And sometimes that difference is in rethinking something completely. And I think that's what you would then call innovation. And we've gone as an industry much beyond that idea of we're just telling the stories of the clients that we work for, to actually creating the stories.

Many faces of innovation

The creativity-innovation nexus has been a focus of research for many years, with scholars attempting to tease out the intricate relationship between the two concepts that are often used interchangeably. Yet, the precise differentiation between creativity and innovation remains elusive. The key reasons lie in their unspecific overapplication[2] and the fact that creativity and innovation are intertwined concepts.[3] However, a distinction between the concepts is clearly visible. If creativity is understood broadly as "the ability to come up with new ideas or solutions to problems"[4] or, as in advertising, novel ways to solve clients' challenges (as discussed in Chapter 1), then, in contrast and by extension, innovation refers to "the generation, acceptance, and implementation of new ideas, processes, products, or services".[5] As Peter Drucker famously explained, "innovation is the specific instrument of entrepreneurship, the means by which change is exploited as an opportunity to differentiate the business or service".[6] Hence, while creativity might be seen as a mental process, innovation could be considered an activity of creative nature that represents intentional, new, and beneficial change aimed at economic growth. The process consists of three phases: (1) the creation or origination of a novel idea,[7] followed by (2) the idea's adoption or diffusion within the economic system,[8] and, finally, (3) its retention, normalcy, and embedding in the economy.[9] Unlike creative processes, innovation causes a structural change in the economic system due to the impact of novel ideas and the implications of their adoption and retention. At the same time, a creative idea is necessary for effective innovation in any product, service, or business process,[10] and in this sense, creativity is a precondition of change and innovation.[11] Creativity, therefore, is the *seed of innovation*.

As creative industries are driven by new ideas and products, innovation is critical to the creative industries as it allows for the *application of creativity*, which, in turn, can lead to increased competitiveness and growth, which are embedded in their "industrial character", linking the act of creation with entrepreneurial and economic activity. Therefore, in advertising, innovation is essential for success. It is not surprising—in a rapidly changing media landscape—creative agencies constantly strive to find (and execute!) new ways to make their client's message audible and distinctive to consumers in the noise of competing brands' marketing. Even though innovation in advertising is popularly characterized by the use of data and technology to create more effective campaigns (like using data-driven targeting to help advertisers more accurately reach their desired audiences or using automation and optimization to buy and sell advertising space), it is important to note that innovation in advertising is not limited to technological advances.[12] New ways of using existing media channels, novel approaches to advertising storytelling, integration of brands, and blurred lines with cultural products are all innovations in this sector as well.[13]

Advertising has long been recognized as a catalyst of innovation across the markets.[14] As it stimulates product development, and it also encourages invention in order to create new products that will be profitable.[15] This gives manufacturers hope that they will recover the costs of product development and turn a profit. Presumably, if a brand had not been able to profit from market stimulation, the manufacturer's enthusiasm for developing new products and service solutions would have subsided. Therefore, it is believed that without advertising, markets would stagnate and innovation would cease. That, in turn, would restrict customer choice and limit their agency.[16] But there is more. In today's media landscape, where fragmentation has created a variety of niche audiences, the supply–demand paradigm paradoxically provides even more "hope" for firms looking to reach smaller target groups.[17] This is because it is becoming increasingly affordable and manageable to target specific audiences through low-cost, agile, or even no-cost (owned) media. As a result, companies (particularly start-ups) are able to thrive and experiment with new content and advertising strategies for longer tails of consumers.[18] In practice, the same investment should have a greater impact or, to put it another way, provide a better return on investment. Consequently, as Nick Kendall, an industry consultant and educator of the next generation of brand specialists, argues, today's media options offer not only "aggressively boosting demand" but also "smart aggressiveness" as they drive supply and demand together. Thus, advertising incentivizes investment in innovation. Simply put, "advertising encourages innovation and so encourages choice". For people, it creates consumer literacy, and so aids choice.[19]

It is important to notice that, as agencies are pressured by the market situation to search for new sources of revenue and ways to monetize their creative potential, they seek to reinvent themselves in relation to clients and other external stakeholders, exceeding the bounds of traditional advertising. The innovation process increasingly considers the development of agencies' new products and services, the establishment of new markets and partnerships, and the consequent changes in the management and organization of creative processes.[20] Therefore, organizational innovativeness—understood as an agency's ability to implement substantial changes in its operational procedures, processing information, workplace structure and culture, and methods for managing external connections[21]—becomes a key ability, which creates new sectoral dynamics and tensions. Consequently, this chapter considers not only selected areas of innovation but also the resulting tensions, such as the visible crises of trust in agencies' ability to innovate in a way that would benefit the clients and the changes in the work environment that practitioners consider essential for both creativity and innovation to thrive.

"Failed" innovations of advertising

Triggered by the reality of connected media ecosystems, the market pressures creative agencies to look for new income streams, and many see the need to reposition themselves by offering a broader scope of services for their clients. They look toward becoming more like business partners than "just" shops for creative outputs. As an executive creative director of a Milan-based boutique agency explains:

> Of course, we need to make sure that our client's communication stands out. And with all the [communication] clutter we have now, we just have to go over the top with what we bring to them [clients and target audiences]. But the brutal truth is that we are quite desperately looking to add extra value and bring more budgets home.

In the swiftly evolving markets of media and consumer goods, no organization can keep up with the ever-changing skills and knowledge needed to generate new goods and solutions alone.[22] Businesses are slowly becoming more open to agencies taking a role in business development processes: not only will they deliver their brand messages but also come up with solutions that could grow their businesses, for example, by coming up with product innovations. This is well reflected in the award categories at advertising (or rather, creative) festivals. Along with innovation awards within medium, channel, or consumer experience categories, the category of "product innovation" has taken dominance as the new "best in show" award. Winning entries take various forms—from inventing a hoverboard that looks and works like one straight out of *Back to the Future*[23] (CHI & Partners[24] for Lexus car manufacturer) to prototyping homes that are capable of withstanding fire, flood, and cyclone (Leo Burnett Sydney for Suncorp insurance company).[25] Meanwhile, it is hard to find award winners who won on the merits of their communication alone.

Even though agencies increasingly innovate their clients' products as part of their services—to loud applause at award shows—the new products are rarely more than buzz-makers. As Szczepaniak critically argued:

> Most of the things winning Cannes Innovation Awards would fail at any major startup event. .... Spectacular solutions are rewarded, but it is more a certain potential, but not the fact that it is really implementable. It is more the promise than tangible solution.

Therefore, more often than not, these products are simply PR stunts without any real consideration for their potential against the real market.

The transformation of creative ideas into tangible and useful products and services is a key problem in innovation management[26] and new venture development.[27] In the case of advertising, the low association between creativity and innovation (for the client's product or business) can be explained by the fact that converting creative ideas into innovations entails, as previously discussed, are two distinct and sometimes antagonistic processes: idea generation and its implementation.[28] Idea generation natively and intuitively finds its place in the creative industries environment as it is intimately linked to exploratory activities[29] that necessitate experimentation, disrupt routines, and challenge conventional assumptions. Idea implementation, on the other hand, is associated with exploitative activities[30] and as such requires a more structured process, efficiency, goal focus, and routine execution. As much as ideas, prototypes, or even limited series consumer products may be delivered by advertising agencies, the sector rarely delivers solutions that can prove their value on the market. Hence, we could easily jump to the conclusion that the advertising sector fails at innovation, as it seems to be unable to implement its ideas. However, considering the actual reasons why clients typically turn to agencies, ideation can be seen as the smallest contribution agencies make to client's success. Instead, innovations (even nonimplementable ones) need to be seen as brand- and image-building tools,[31] making the adoption and retention constitute the central value. Therefore, the innovative potential of the creative industries is to create consumer demand for new goods,[32] which is the end goal of the process. We can then argue that the advertising industry, in fact, excels at delivering all three stages of the innovation trajectory: origination, adoption, and retention.

In its role of brand building and creating demand for products, advertising's innovative power is frequently not in developing technological or channel innovations but rather in linking previously unconnected ideas or helping innovations achieve visibility and the ability to reach broader markets. Rarely does the sector itself invent a new technological solution, which is not within the scope of its business competencies. Rather, it has an eye for inventions across various markets, brings them to the public view, offers the ground (and budget) for testing and experimentation, and triggers broader discussion. As Korsten reflects:

> If you try to look that [AI-centered software solutions] up on the Microsoft website, it's not very appealing. But if you think about an idea, like the Next Rembrandt, where you take that technology and you wrap it into something that people find very interesting to engage with, then it might become something with a broader appeal and easier to adopt for a broader audience. . . . I give them some love and attention.

An example of a technology that was brought to the public eye through advertising is the virtual reality headset, which was originally developed for gaming purposes and has since been adapted for use in other areas, such as healthcare and education. Advertising played a role in raising awareness of technology and building mainstream appeal. In 2015, *The New York Times* created a marketing campaign that included a VR app and a film directed by VRSE. works' Imraan Ismail and *The New York Times'* Ben Solomon (who was a part of the *Times* team that won the Pulitzer Prize for International Reporting in 2015 for front-line reporting about Ebola in Africa).[33] Called *The Displaced*, the 11-minute film chronicles the experiences of three refugee children from some of the most war-ravaged regions on Earth. By mailing out 1.1 million Google Cardboard headsets to their print subscribers, *The New York Times* brought a niche technology to the mass market on an unprecedented scale. Jenna Pirog, a *New York Times* contributing editor who creates VR videos, explained in an interview for Nieman News that her team was pleasantly surprised by the audience's reaction:

> We really didn't know what the reaction would be. There's so much onboarding associated with this film. You have to find your cardboard viewer in your Sunday paper, and download the app, and download the film, and trust us and put your phone in the Cardboard viewer, and get your headphones on. But we were just blown away by the response.[34]

Even though this innovation is arguably more about journalism than advertising, the entry made its case as a promotional campaign. Jury president Jae Goodman explained during the postshow press conference: "The creation of the NYT VR app—that in and of itself catapults *The New York Times* [as a brand], known as the Grey Lady, in our opinion, 100 years forward".[35]

Innovating while nobody believes

As previously discussed, the purpose of innovative projects in advertising is usually linked to creating buzz around the brand, delivering a message to consumers, differentiating from other brands on the market, arousing public interest, and increasing the image and prestige of the brand.[36] Even though the benefits of innovating and delivering creative solutions seem to be clear for brands, clients oftentimes hesitate to give a green light to bold and novel ideas by their creative partners. Bas Korsten admits that, even though the client asked to connect art and culture sponsorship with the innovative nature of their business, they did not initially want to go ahead with the idea of the Next Rembrandt:

> When I presented the idea to ING, they said, "Well, no, we don't want to do this. We want to give a gift to the Rijksmuseum as sort of a celebration of our partnership. And we don't know if the idea of this painting is ever going to be something interesting or good, so we don't want to buy a gift that we don't know if it's going to be a good gift." So, I said, "Well, okay, I can see that." But I knew somewhere that this idea needed to see the light of day.

Thus, the agency kept pushing, working on the project within its own resources, partnering with Microsoft, and going ahead with the it without the client's involvement. Only when it was about 80% complete, with a clear sense of how it would look, they did go back to ING and get the project approved.

Similarly, dentsuACHTUNG!'s Mervyn Ten Dam recalls working on one of their most awarded campaigns. Volkswagen, the German car manufacturer, was one of the most popular automobile brands in the Netherlands for decades. Even though Volkswagen is often considered a family vehicle brand, the company asked its agency to come up with a unique strategy to develop brand sympathy among families in order to sustain scores on crucial brand values and show the innovativeness of the company. The creative team worked around the somewhat obvious, yet equally relevant consumer insight that seven out of ten children use screens during long trips, making them fixated on devices and oblivious to their surroundings. Most parents, however, feel bad about that, as they believe that family drives are an ideal time for bonding and an opportunity to encourage their children to open up.

As a result, the team searched for ideas to design an experience that aimed at reducing screen time in the car, sparking children's imagination, and making interaction in the vehicle easier. They developed *Road Tales* (or rather *Snel-weg Sprookjes*), a form of location-based audiobooks set in specific locations that turn roadways and objects around them into engaging stories. To do this, the team behind the campaign scanned the complete Dutch highway system (5000 kilometers) to detect thousands of objects along the motorways. As a next step, they collaborated with a number of artists and award-winning children's book authors (borrowing expertise from another creative sector) to create a storytelling experience that felt both unique and personal. The experience was accessible through an app that parents could connect to the car's sound system to play an interactive narrative and then put the phone aside, making children engaged in high-quality stories off-screen, and making travel itself more vivid and exciting.[37]

Ten Dam recalls the process that they went through with the client:

> They didn't believe in it. They believed in one of the other ideas more. And we believed in this idea better. [So,] we made a little demo, starting from their main office. So, we just took a few objects, we asked the voiceover to speak. And we had to put the marketing director literally in the backseat of the Volkswagen, even giving him some candies that we bought for the travel. And that's how we convinced him he was going to do this.

Those situations are not unique. When talking to creative leads about the bravest and most innovative works that they have realized in recent years, a striking theme recurs like a chorus: first, the client did not like or rejected the idea, and it took much work to convince them otherwise. Some creatives link these difficulties with the fact that, in the market in which they operate, there is no traditional space for the exploration and development of new ideas because they need to work within the clients' limited budgets, and clients are often only willing to spend on "proven" solutions. Other examples show the issue of a lack of confidence in convincing key stakeholders to implement highly creative solutions. As the State of Creativity 2022 report by Cannes Lions indicates, 29% of brands and 24% of agencies feel very or extremely confident in convincing their CFOs or clients, respectively, to invest in high-quality creativity, while only 15% of agencies feel highly confident in their clients' ability to apply commercially successful creativity.[38]

However, not everyone believes in pushing hard and going the extra mile to convince clients to buy innovative ideas. "There is no persuasion. I spend a lot of time and energy on working and connecting with people that I know are open to this type of thing and do not waste my energy selling the boldest ideas to people I know that there will be no strong support from them, nor their organizations; they wouldn't be brave enough to do such things" says Szczepaniak. He continues, "the second level is inspiring, not educating, but inspiring others. There, we convince that it is worth trying, it is worth looking for bolder ways. And it works". Szczepaniak led the team responsible for the Grand Prix winning campaign for the Glass Lion for Change, an award that "celebrates culture-shifting creativity".[39] The campaign, The Last Ever Issue, was a special issue of *Your Weekend* (originally, *Twój Weekend*), Poland's most popular adult magazine, with a circulation of over 50,000 copies per issue. In December 2018, the title became available for sale and was immediately bought by the agency together with three brands, two clients of VMLY&R, and one news portal. The collaborating partners bought it to publish one more issue, transforming *Your Weekend* into a conversation-sparking magazine that promoted diverse and progressive narratives of femininity and confronted the culture of sexism and gender inequality. The last issue sales made it the best-selling issue of the magazine in ten years. Szczepaniak explains the process of onboarding clients to the campaign:

> There was no need to convince anyone to do so. It took maybe an hour to come up with the idea and after an hour, we already had the consent of the first brand that said it was going into it. No presentations; phone-call decision. We reached out to people whom we knew would be ready to do such a thing.

Clearly, innovation in advertising is linked not only to the capabilities of creative teams but also to brand attitudes toward creative advertising,[40] their openness to new ideas, and willingness to take risks,[41] which, in turn, links to the organization's internal culture, approach, and processes.[42] Last but not least is an agency's ability to manage its stakeholders and engage people, organizations, and brands.[43] Scholars have argued that formal and informal mechanisms of governance act as complements to innovation in the sector.[44] The joint activities between the agency and its clients are often articulated on the basis of formal procedures, predesigned processes, and quite rigid schemes like workflows, which are built to take into account both the agency's and the client's contributions to the production process.[45] The crucial function of the account managers and directors is to act as gatekeepers for the interaction between the agency and the client.[46] This links to some issues that arise for both creatives and clients: the strict structure—on both hierarchical and procedural levels—limits the agency's ability to involve the client in roles of co-diagnoser, co-designer, co-producer, co-implementor, co-marketer, and co-developer[47] and, therefore, hurts open communication and space for innovation.

Client–agency relationship models are the subject of extensive research that explores single, multi, and dedicated agency models, their dynamics, and management.[48] However, the difficulty of executing creative ideas in the increasingly fragmented market suggests limited confidence that creative teams alone can drive business effectiveness. Especially, within smaller, boutique agencies, where the service is oriented toward advising and problem solving,[49] the rigid sequestration of creative work inside the agency is increasingly released in favor of greater input from the client. As Greg Hanh, a founder and chief creative officer at Mischief—an agency named A-List 2022 #1 by AdAge[50]—explained:

> All the way from when I started in advertising, there was always this, "don't show them until it's ready"; "Don't show them until you know it's been approved." It doesn't have to be perfect when we bring it to people. We have a phrase that we use in some of our conversations with our clients is that we're not like the Tada! agency, we're the Aha! Agency. We will come and bring you little insights along the way. Versus the big show and reveal at the end. The clients are experts in a lot of stuff.[51]

Similarly, as the executive creative director of a Sydney-based independent creative agency explained:

> The issue with many network agencies is that the agency pitches to the client. Client likes what he sees and chooses the agency. But it was the last time he saw this team. It is because the agency took what they believed were their best people to win the client, but somebody else will be handling the account. This is unbelievable to me. We need to trust each other. And how can we build the trust if we open like that?

Some declare going as far as choosing clients based on "chemistry", values alignment, and personal preference: "We don't take on clients we don't like as people", as Hanh expressed.[52] Others invest time to seed curiosity and a can-do-better attitude in clients, who are assessed based on their potential for giving the space to deliver innovative work, as earlier pointed out by Szczepaniak.

Aiming for the impossible

Why would creative agencies push so badly for innovation and state-of-the-art creative work, with massive investments of their own resources but no promise of return? It may have something to do with the creatives' egos that push for award-winning campaigns and have a need for creative expression, but there seem to be more pragmatic reasons, too. The ranking of creative agencies in various major advertising competitions, such as Cannes Lions, the One Show, Clio Awards, The Drum, and others, is a significant consideration affecting brand decisions,[53] which, in turn, means that these events function as a screening mechanism for businesses to select the best agency for them. These shows and festivals can be an important tool for agencies to build their reputation and attract more clients. Consequently, enhancing the creativity of their work is a practical strategy for them to build their businesses.

Also important in today's industry climate is the fact that winning an award can also help to attract and retain top talent. Potential employees will be attracted to an agency with a proven record of success, and the awards can help an increasing problem of bringing new creative power. Moreover, as Bas Korsten explains, awards and buzz were not directly the most satisfying outcomes for him in the case of the Next Rembrandt. It was how the project empowered his team and fueled its future work:

> I come to learn that creativity is a lot about self-confidence. And actually, believing in an idea is half the job. So, I think these projects helped to instill confidence in the whole of the agency, that anything is possible. Which is an invaluable mindset to have in a creative agency. Because if you believe in your own idea, then you walk up bits harder when you go into the meeting room, and you're willing to go a bit harder on the client, when he says no. And if you believe in an idea, I think it's almost your duty, to not let anyone stop you in bringing it to life. I think that's what it does. I think it fuels that confidence.

In this sense, recognition for creativity (and innovation, understood as implementing creativity into specific executable projects) can help an agency to motivate and manage its creative power, especially considering advertising a job, where creatives constantly need to seek approval from clients and accounts. The recognition becomes a quality mark and a factor contributing to building the creative identity of the talent.[54] Industry awards are a great way to gain peer appreciation and professional networking as they demonstrate that the winner adheres to ideals that are more important than those of the advertising industry as a whole. In addition, unlike regular day-to-day employment, creative rewards are permanent, and the plaque or trophy signifies "creative permanence".[55]

Making space for innovation

Alex Jenkins, editor of *Contagious Magazine*, puts it succinctly when he recalls a customer telling him, "I didn't want to pay for my agencies to experiment and develop as often as I needed them to".[56] It is clear that there are challenges that agencies face when it comes to innovation. Many creative agencies struggle to develop an innovation pipeline and provide their clients with novel solutions on a regular and larger scale. One of the biggest challenges pointed to by practitioners is clients' overall disinterest in finding bold and untypical solutions. The problem can be linked to the fact that brand and marketing managers are also accounting for the results against relatively short periods or limited marketing budgets. Both result in the lack of time and resources that clients are willing to invest in innovation. There is also a lot of pressure put on the agencies to deliver results quickly, which means that they need to be able to show clients developed propositions together with the value of innovation quickly and effectively. Finally, there is the challenge of general skepticism toward innovation as delivered by agencies, as discussed earlier. As experts have pointed out, the potential for resolving issues in order to enable innovation is present even in the face of limited initial resources. Structural and cultural appointments that are independent of such attachment can, in their view, pave the way for innovation to take place.

Establishing senior leadership for innovation

Some experts, like Daniele Fiandaca, point out that it is essential for agencies to have a board-level member responsible for innovation in order for it to be successful.[57] They point to a lack of responsibility for innovation at the senior level as one of the main reasons why organizations struggle to be innovative since many see this work as the domain of mid-level staff or "innovation teams". This means that innovation can be easily overlooked or sidelined when it comes to decision-making and budgeting. What is needed is a clear commitment from the senior team that innovation is a priority, and they are willing to drive the necessary changes to give innovation visibility and importance. On the other hand, some argue that innovation should not happen in isolation or silos, but everyone in the agency should have an opportunity to innovate within their respective domains. When a single person in an agency is solely responsible for innovation, they are often disconnected from the everyday work of the company. In practice, an appointed "innovation" person may only be engaged with projects the agency perceives as strategic or plans to present at an industry conference and may have limited ability to inspire teams working on day-to-day projects. As a result, they may be more the "face" of innovation than the actual driving force. What is interesting, previous studies on the role of top management found that independent boards of directors were associated with a higher rate of corporate innovation.[58] Furthermore, a study by Hambrick and Mason[59] showed that top management teams with a strong commitment to their original resources were less likely to pursue innovative strategies, which suggests that establishing senior leadership for innovation may not be sufficient if those individuals are still wedded to the status quo.

Building a culture that invites creativity and innovation

While responsibility for innovation might reside with someone senior, for an agency to embrace innovation, it needs to permeate throughout the agency, which requires a specific organizational culture. Many creatives consider innovation to be a blend of exploration and experimentation, a fun and playful activity that they enjoy. Therefore, it is key for the agencies to create an environment that gives internal and external motivation, would fuel "passion" and support "wanting to" over "having to" attitudes.[60] Thus, being

involved in developing novel ideas, innovative, and first-of-their-kind projects can serve as a tool for fueling creativity and motivating talent to push
themselves more. "It's funny that some of my favorite projects are those that
never got green light. I still love them [laughter]. And I have them in a folder
'too cool to be done'", explains a creative director of one of the London-
based network agencies. Korsten explains that he also sees a business value
in his team to work on innovative ideas even (or especially) when they are
not directly related to current client work:

> I just keep them on a separate track. You couldn't make a living on this.
> But they could inspire the work that you're doing for your clients in the
> future. So that's why I keep doing that and keep pushing myself to put
> energy into those projects [that are done outside the scope of what was
> requested by the clients].

Simultaneously, there is a need to foster an agile culture, as agencies operate in an ever-changing environment in which flexibility, reactiveness, and
adaptability are keys. In order to encourage an environment that is conducive
to innovation, practitioners believe that it is important to give employees the
freedom to explore new ideas and tools, and to invite explorative approaches.
By doing so, agencies can create an environment in which employees feel
comfortable taking risks and trying new things. This notion also appears in
academic research that supports the idea that a flexible workplace culture is
necessary for fostering innovation. For example, a study by Malik and colleagues found that agile work practices were associated with higher levels
of creativity and innovation.[61] In addition, a study by Sanna Ketonen-Oksi
on digitalized, service-based working cultures[62] recognizes innovation-related
creativity as a skill that we all naturally possess and should be developed with
the support of the workplace. Therefore, innovation should be seen as a feature that builds on both personal mastery of the employee's thought processes
and behavioral patterns in relation to their own capacities for creativity and
innovation (such as building creative confidence, mentioned by Korsten)
and the organizations' capacity to foster employee growth in both individual and
team-based creative and innovative capacities. Hence, even though it might
sound obvious and easily implementable, in order to foster innovation, agencies need to create a workplace culture that is open to change and provides
employees with the opportunity to explore new ideas.

Finding time outside tight deadlines and ensuring budget for innovation

What becomes clear is that the primary barrier to innovation is typically "time
and money"—that is, the amount of time required to generate new ideas and
the resources necessary to bring them to fruition. It becomes increasingly

important for agencies to have a dedicated innovation budget that is not directly tied to any client account but rather is set exclusively for research and development. As information technologies are always evolving, consequently, there is always a need for new information skillsets. Agencies need to keep investing in these areas not only to maintain their competitive advantage, optimize their creative output, and stay ahead of the curve when it comes to offering innovative solutions to clients but also in order to nurture their creative talent. As the managing director of a Helsinki-based agency explained:

> Let's say I hired a CD [creative director] 15 years ago. And he still is in the agency. Think about how world has changed over those years. How can I expect people to keep up with all tech and science and educate juniors? If I don't invest, they will stay in the TV or Facebook era forever.

Many creatives point out that the fast-paced nature of the industry makes it difficult for them to find time for innovation or to keep a pipeline of "sideprojects" as they are constantly pressured by increasingly tight deadlines: "[the creatives] hardly get the headspace to work on exceptional ideas"[63]; "there is oppressive need for speed"[64]; and "we need time: time to process the problem, time to think about solutions, time to evaluate ideas, and time to execute these creative solutions".[65] Others point out that there is a need for developing new ways of working, as the collaborative approach to creative work, compared to the siloed work of creative teams, has been found to be more effective. Dawid Szczepaniak explained his approach to managing creative teams: "what used to be 2–3 days is today one hour, but I see this 1-hour time of the right people at the table [as] more effective than 2–3 days of a creative team sitting and contemplating". This is likely due to the collaborative nature of the process, which allows for different people with different skills and perspectives to come together to create something that is greater than the sum of its parts; they are able to build off of each other. As will be discussed further in the following chapters, the collaborative work models known in other creative industries, such as film, slowly become an area of interest for the advertising industry as well, but not only in the context of efficiency.

Notes

1 Based on information received from the agency and existing press releases.
2 Hartley, J., Potts, J., Cunningham, S., Flew, T., Keane, M., & Banks, J. (2013). *Key concepts in creative industries*. Sage.
3 Tang, M., & Werner, C. H. (2017). *Handbook of the management of creativity and innovation: Theory and practice*. World Scientific.
4 Amabile, T. (2018). *Creativity in context: Update to the social psychology of creativity*. Routledge.
5 Thompson, V. A. (1965). Bureaucracy and innovation. *Administrative Science Quarterly*, *10*(1). https://doi.org/10.2307/2391646.

6 Drucker, P. F. (2015). *Innovation and entrepreneurship*. Routledge.

7 von Hippel, E. (2007). *The sources of innovation*. Oxford University Press.

8 Rogers, E. M. (2005). *Diffusion of innovations*. Free Press.

9 Drucker, P. F. (2015). *Innovation and entrepreneurship*. Routledge.

10 Amabile, T. M., Conti, R., Coon, H., Lazenby, J., & Herron, M. (1996). Assessing the work environment for creativity. *Academy of Management Journal*, *39*(5), 1154–1184. https://doi.org/10.5465/256995; Baer, J. (2012). Domain specificity and the limits of creativity theory. *The Journal of Creative Behavior*, *46*(1), 16–29. https://doi.org/10.1002/jocb.002.

11 Styhre, A., & Sundgren, M. (2005). *Managing creativity in organisations. Critique and practice*. Palgrave Macmillan; Kilbourne, L. M., & Woodman, R. W. (1999). Barriers to organizational creativity. In A. Montuori & R. E. Purser (Eds.), *Social creativity in organizations* (pp. 125–150). Hampton Press.

12 Mendelová, D., & Zausková, A. (2015). Innovation in the Slovak advertising environment. *Communication Today*, *6*(1).

13 Mas-Manchón, L. (Ed.). (2022). *Innovation in advertising and branding communication*. Routledge.

14 Borden, N. H. (1976). *The economic effects of advertising*. Arno Press.

15 Boier, R. (2014). Marketing and innovation—a relationship approach. *Studies and Scientific Researches. Economics Edition*, (20). https://doi.org/10.29358/sceco.v0i20.267; Kumar, V., & Gupta, S. (2016). Conceptualizing the evolution and future of advertising. *Journal of Advertising*, *45*(3), 302–317. https://doi.org/10.1080/009 13367.2016.1199335.

16 Borden, N. H. (1976). *The economic effects of advertising*. Arno Press.

17 Kendall, N. (2021, August 25). How does advertising affect innovation, quality & consumer choice? *Advertising Association*. Retrieved September 16, 2022, from https://adassoc.org.uk/credos/how-does-advertising-affect-innovation-quality-and-consumer-choice/.

18 The "long tail" is a business term for the phenomena of a large number of unique items selling in small quantities. This contrasts with the traditional business model, which focuses on a smaller number of high-volume items. Chris Anderson first proposed the long tail theory in an October 2004 article in Wired magazine. Anderson's article cited examples such as Amazon, eBay, and Apple's iTunes Store, which offer a very large number of products for sale, most of which sell in low volumes. Anderson argued that the long tail was made possible by the internet, which allows businesses to reach consumers directly and efficiently. The same logic can be applied to communication—instead of reaching mass audiences, digital means allow for relatively precise targeting of messages to numerous varied audiences. Anderson, C. (2004, October 1). The long tail. *Wired*. Retrieved September 16, 2022, from www.wired.com/2004/10/tail/.

19 Kendall, N. (2021, August 25). How does advertising affect innovation, quality & consumer choice? *Advertising Association*. Retrieved September 16, 2022, from https://adassoc.org.uk/credos/how-does-advertising-affect-innovation-quality-and-consumer-choice/.

20 Mendelová, D., & Zausková, A. (2015). Innovation in the Slovak advertising environment. *Communication Today*, *6*(1).

21 Cruz-Cunha, M. M., & Putnik, G. (2008). *Encyclopedia of networked and virtual organizations*. Information Science Reference.

22 Gulati, R. (1995). Does familiarity breed trust? The implications of repeated ties for contractual choice in alliances. *Academy of Management Journal*, *38*(1), 85–112. https://doi.org/10.5465/256729; Hung, S.-C. (2002). Mobilising networks to achieve strategic difference. *Long Range Planning*, *35*(6), 591–613. https://doi.org/10.1016/s0024-6301(02)00150-4.

23 Eurobest. (2015). 2015 Promo & activation. *Eurobest*. Retrieved September 16, 2022, from https://www2.eurobest.com/winners/2015/promo/entry.cfm?entryid=2580&award=99&order=3&direction=2.

24 Now The & Partnership.

25 Leo Burnett. (2021). Leo Burnett Sydney and Suncorp battle extreme weather with "one house to save many". *Leo Burnett Worldwide*. Retrieved September 16, 2022, from https://leoburnett.com/news/leo-burnett-sydney-and-suncorp-battle-extreme-weather-with-one-house-to-save-many.

26 Van de Ven, A. H. (1986). Central problems in the management of innovation. *Management Science*, *32*(5), 590–607. https://doi.org/10.1287/mnsc.32.5.590.

27 Drucker, P. F. (1998). The discipline of innovation. *Leader to Leader*, *1998*(9), 13–15. https://doi.org/10.1002/ltl.40619980906.

28 Rosing, K., Frese, M., & Bausch, A. (2011). Explaining the heterogeneity of the leadership-innovation relationship: Ambidextrous leadership. *The Leadership Quarterly*, *22*(5), 956–974. https://doi.org/10.1016/j.leaqua.2011.07.014.

29 Ibid.

30 Ibid; Exploitative activities may be understood here as for example refinement of existing routines to develop new products or the refinement of existing routines to offer new products to customers. Tabeau, K., Gemser, G., Hultink, E. J., & Wijnberg, N. M. (2016). Exploration and exploitation activities for design innovation. *Journal of Marketing Management*, *33*(3–4), 203–225. https://doi.org/10.1080/0267257x.2016.1195855.

31 Mas-Manchón, L. (Ed.). (2022). *Innovation in advertising and branding communication*. Routledge.

32 Hartley, J., Potts, J., Cunningham, S., Flew, T., Keane, M., & Banks, J. (2013). *Key concepts in creative industries*. Sage.

33 The Pulitzer Prizes. (2015). The 2015 Pulitzer Prize winner in international reporting—the New York Times staff. *The Pulitzer Prizes*. Retrieved September 16, 2022, from www.pulitzer.org/winners/new-york-times-staff.

34 Roush, W. (2019, February 27). Jenna Pirog on virtual reality in "the displaced." *Nieman Foundation*. Retrieved September 16, 2022, from https://nieman.harvard.edu/stories/annotation-tuesday-jenna-pirog-on-virtual-reality-in-the-displaced/.

35 Nudd, T. (2016, June 24). The New York Times VR film 'the displaced' wins the Lions Entertainment grand prix. *Adweek*. Retrieved September 16, 2022, from www.adweek.com/brand-marketing/new-york-times-vr-film-displaced-wins-lions-entertainment-grand-prix-172225/.

36 Mas-Manchón, L. (Ed.). (2022). *Innovation in advertising and branding communication*. Routledge.

37 Based on information received from the agency and existing press releases.

38 Cannes Lions. (2022). (rep.). *State of creativity 2022*. Cannes Lions.

39 Cannes Lions. (2022). Glass: The lion for change. *Cannes Lions*. Retrieved September 16, 2022, from www.canneslions.com/enter/awards/good/glass-the-lion-for-change.

40 Kilgour, M., Sasser, S., & Koslow, S. (2013). Creativity awards: Great expectations? *Creativity Research Journal*, *25*(2), 163–171. https://doi.org/10.1080/10400419.2013.783741.

41 Whiteside, S., & Tiltman, D. (2013). Warc trends: The innovation casebook—explore the world's freshest communications ideas. *Warc*. Retrieved September 16, 2022, from www.warc.com/content/article/warc-trends/warc-trends-the-innovation-casebook-explore-the-worlds-freshest-communications-ideas/en-gb/99872.

42 Blank, S. (2019, October 7). Why companies do "innovation theater" instead of actual innovation. *Harvard Business Review*. Retrieved September 16, 2022, from https://hbr.org/2019/10/why-companies-do-innovation-theater-instead-of-

actual-innovation?utm_medium=social&utm_campaign=hbr&utm_source=LinkedIn&tpcc=orgsocial_edit.

43 Sheehan, K. B., & Morrison, D. K. (2009). The creativity challenge. *Journal of Interactive Advertising*, *9*(2), 40–43. https://doi.org/10.1080/15252019.2009.10722154.

44 Poppo, L., & Zenger, T. (2002). Do formal contracts and relational governance function as substitutes or complements? *Strategic Management Journal*, *23*(8), 707–725. https://doi.org/10.1002/smj.249.

45 Zeithaml, V. A., Bitner, M. J., & Gremler, D. (2013). *Services marketing: Integrating customer focus across the firm*. McGraw-Hill.

46 Grabher, G. (2002). The project ecology of advertising: Tasks, talents and teams. *Regional Studies*, *36*(3), 245–262. https://doi.org/10.1080/00343400220122052.

47 Aarikka-Stenroos, L., & Jaakkola, E. (2012). Value co-creation in knowledge intensive business services: A dyadic perspective on the joint problem solving process. *Industrial Marketing Management*, *41*(1), 15–26. https://doi.org/10.1016/j.indmarman.2011.11.008.

48 For example: Halinen, A. (2002). *Relationship marketing in professional services a study of agency-client dynamics in the advertising sector*. Routledge; Michell, P. C. N., & Sanders, N. H. (1995). Loyalty in agency-client relations: The impact of the organizational context. *Journal of Advertising Research*, *35*(2), 9–22; Tena, M. E. (2014). *Ad agency-client relationship models: Advantages and disadvantages*. Universidad de Navarra.

49 Bolton, R., & Saxena-Iyer, S. (2009). Interactive services: A framework, synthesis and research directions. *Journal of Interactive Marketing*, *23*(1), 91–104. https://doi.org/10.1016/j.intmar.2008.11.002.

50 Diaz, A.-C. (2022, March 14). Mischief @ no fixed address soared with fearless ideas, sharp strategy and an ego-free M.O. *Ad Age*. Retrieved September 17, 2022, from https://adage.com/article/special-report-agency-list/list-2022-best-agency-mischief/2403881.

51 Bonke, A., & Bonke, C. (Directors). (2022). *Kill your darlings* [Film]. Drive Studios.

52 Ibid.

53 Kübler, R. V., & Proppe, D. (2012). Faking or convincing: Why do some advertising campaigns win creativity awards? *Business Research*, *5*(1), 60–81. https://doi.org/10.1007/bf03342732.

54 Hackley, C., & Kover, A. J. (2007). The trouble with creatives: Negotiating creative identity in advertising agencies. *International Journal of Advertising*, *26*(1), 63–78. https://doi.org/10.1080/02650487.2007.11072996.

55 Ibid.

56 Fiandaca, D. (2014). Role of innovation within advertising. In D. Fiandaca, A. Andjelic, & G. Kay (Eds.), *Hacker, maker, teacher, thief: Advertising's next generation* (pp. 165–172). Creative Social.

57 Compare: Fiandaca, D. (2014). Role of innovation within advertising. In D. Fiandaca, A. Andjelic, & G. Kay (Eds.), *Hacker, maker, teacher, thief: Advertising's next generation* (pp. 165–172). Creative Social.

58 Balsmeier, B., Fleming, L., & Manso, G. (2017). Independent boards and innovation. *Journal of Financial Economics*, *123*(3), 536–557. https://doi.org/10.1016/j.jfineco.2016.12.005.

59 Hambrick, D. C., & Mason, P. A. (1984). Upper echelons: The organization as a reflection of its top managers. *Academy of Management Review*, *9*(2), 193–206. https://doi.org/10.5465/amr.1984.4277628.

60 Fisher, R., & Williams, M. (2013). *Unlocking creativity: Teaching across the curriculum*. Routledge.

61 Malik, M., Sarwar, S., & Orr, S. (2021). Agile practices and performance: Examining the role of psychological empowerment. *International Journal of Project Management, 39*(1), 10–20. https://doi.org/10.1016/j.ijproman.2020.09.002.
62 Ketonen-Oksi, S. (2017). Re-inventing organizational creativity and innovation through adopting a service-based working culture. In G. Schiuma & A. Lerro (Eds.), *Integrating art and creativity into business practice* (pp. 1–21). Business Science Reference.
63 Ibid.
64 Cannes Lions. (2022). (rep.). *State of creativity 2022*. Cannes Lions.
65 Ibid.

3   Advertising X entertainment

The power of stories

We all have stories that our families pass down, that cycle through generations. And regardless of what you think is true, or what you have to do with it, you remember those stories. You know what those stories represent. You can kind of identify people based on the stories. And as a brand, you got to lean into that model. You can't just be about information. You got to have some story, a character.

If you're selling a detergent to make cleaner clothes, there's a person, a householder, who needs to clean clothes. And there's a reason he does it: because you are going to a new job interview and need to be clean and fresh to make an impression. Is it because you have people visiting your house and wash all the sheets and towels to be a great host. There's a story behind why and a brand is ultimately about a person, because it's a consumer that needs it.[1]

The use of narratives in advertisements is a well-established technique that traces back to the early days of modern advertising.[2] This is not surprising, given the narrative's proven effectiveness at conveying information[3] and making an emotional connection with the audience.[4] During the late 1990s, narrative advertising constituted roughly a quarter of all ads aired on television.[5] However, the 1990s were also a time when advertising seemed to be a relatively simple business.[6] On any given day, we might have watched over four hours of television.[7] The "push" advertising of TV commercials focused on exposing a "unique selling proposition"[8] and effectively but bluntly presenting whatever marketers considered to be "unique" about their product or valuable for the consumer.[9] Heading toward the 2000s, however, the media landscape was gaining complexity. A dynamically exploding TV market was making audiences jump from channel to channel, making them more difficult to catch with an ad message. DVR technology allowed for fast-forwarding through ads. The rising accessibility and popularization of the Internet were taking eyes away from the TV set. Technology disrupting was no longer as effective as it used to be, while the costs of reaching audiences through the media sector and TV spots were only rising. The most significant change was visible as a

DOI: 10.4324/9781003263128-4

shift of power from those who produce and distribute entertainment to people who actually consume it.[10] A prime example of this change was the shift from record labels to streaming services. Record labels used to have full control over what music was produced and how it was distributed. They would sign artists and produce their albums, which they then shipped off to stores for people to purchase. However, with the rise of streaming services, such as Spotify and Apple Music, people are now able to listen to whatever they want and whenever they want, and it is no different for TV programming or advertising. The consumer of the first decade of 2000s has more power and freedom, and it has profound implications for industries, which have long relied on their control over the means of production and distribution to maintain their profitability. As Procter & Gamble's then global marketing officer, Jim Stengel, claimed at an industry event in 2004, "there must be—and is—life beyond the 30-second TV spot".[11] A clear need for action was arising, but there was no clarity on how to proceed.

In the early 2000s, marketers were starting to get the idea that they needed to keep the client interested, engaged, and entertained.[12] As a result, they had slowly begun to shift their focus from mass exposure to niche markets and to create more compelling content that people actually wanted to consume, despite being advertisements. Brands started looking for space somewhere within the entertainment that their audiences consume. Product placement— or in the industry jargon a brand integration—became more sophisticated, becoming a popular means to associate brands with specific content and reach wider audiences through visual media. Along with the growth of the entertainment industry, spending on product placement reached a record number of $4.25 billion in 2005 alone.[13] At the same time, the way brands worked with studios also began to evolve. As Elliott notes,[14] in the past, advertisers would wait until a show or movie franchise became a hit before attempting to place their products in it. In the 2000s, however, advertising deals were increasingly being struck at the development stage, giving advertisers exclusive rights, reduced competition, and the ability to organically incorporate products into scenes. This shift also marked more seamless product integration, as scenes could be written from the beginning with a particular brand in mind, instead of added "on top" of already existing scripts and concepts. Another factor was the increase in reality television, where the absence of scripts and emphasis on scenarios from "real life" were making it easy to incorporate products and brand names.[15]

In the countries where regulations allowed it, brands tried to get more visibility in prime-time television by developing their own broadcast content in cooperation with TV stations. In many ways, these strategies seem similar to the advertising of the 1930s radio dramas and 1950s TV shows, such as the renowned Colgate Comedy Hour and Kraft Television Theater,[16] where brands sponsored radio and TV programming in exchange for product mentions. However, it has again become imperative for marketers to understand how to produce more engaging and entertaining content. For example, TBWA\ Helsinki offered Finnish audiences of the country's biggest commercial broadcaster MTV3 a sitcom ironically titled Brändärit,[17] which can be translated as *Buy This*. This scripted show told the story of a fictional ad agency, which was working with some of TBWA's real clients to produce TV spots. The audience could follow the trials and tribulations of a fictionalized creative process, seasoned, naturally, and with numerous gags. However, the "fictional" commercials were actually produced and aired directly after the show. This not only managed to embed branded messaging into prime-time programming but also actually made audiences want to see the commercial break—viewers stayed for the commercials in over 70% of cases.[18] As Juha-Matti Raunio, agency lead and one of the minds behind Brändärit, explained after the campaign won Grand Prix Entertainment at the 2014 Eurobest festival:

> For brands, entertainment is an essentially an untapped medium for telling meaningful stories to a broad audience. Advertising's attention values [measures of audience attention] are declining year after year, while the need for high-quality content is soaring. And when it's done right, it is resulting in a win-win situation for both customers and brands.[19]

In 2014, Lego came to the forefront of branded entertainment, creating the "hybrid film", *The Lego Movie*, a computer-animated adventure-comedy directed and written by Phil Lord and Christopher Miller, combined with advertising. Based on the Lego line of construction toys, the film tells the story of an ordinary Lego minifigure who finds himself prophesied to save the world from a tyrannical business magnate who plans to glue everything in the Lego world into one homogeneous piece. *The Lego Movie*'s success comes in offering every piece of the current branding puzzle, including surface-level subversion. Not only does the film creatively praise its own vast, diversified, and endless universe but it also celebrates the value of play and creativity while mocking the faux positivity of current corporate schlock (as in the original song, "Everything is fantastic!" that, incidentally, was nominated for an Oscar).[20] A major marketing challenge for the Lego team is to make their products exciting to children (their core target group for the majority of blocks lines) though it is adults who control home budgets and make purchases. This is something that the movie also addressed—while the Lego Movie is thrilling entertainment for kids, it is still appealing to adults.[21] All things considered, the movie became a rare example of brand work that gained the honest interest of audiences, who not only expressed the wish to watch this 101-minute commercial but also bought regular-priced cinema tickets to see it, resulting in $468,266,122 worldwide gross ticket sales.[22] Moreover, the brand experienced a sales jump of 14% in 2014 after the release of the movie[23] and 25% in 2015,[24] demonstrating that brands can deliver Hollywood-quality entertainment that consumers are willing to pay for. The approach has pushed the boundaries of what is possible in terms of branded content and taken the concept of branded entertainment to a whole new level.

However, Lego was not the only one tapping into the idea of telling stories outside the 30-second ad format. In the Real Beauty Sketches campaign, for example, Dove aimed to show women how beautiful they are based on the compliments of others. Producers asked a number of women to describe themselves to a sketch artist and then had a stranger describe them as well. The video spread over the Internet with over 60 million views on YouTube.[25] In Red Bull's Stratos campaign, Felix Baumgartner, an Austrian skydiver, jumped from "space" (or, rather, the stratosphere's altitude of about 39 kilometers or 24 miles). This feat set the world record in skydiving and made him the first man to break the sound barrier relative to the surface without the assistance of a vehicle. His attempt was followed by 9.5 million people live on YouTube.[26] Or consider Chipotle, with its stop-motion short film *Back to the Start*, which follows the story of a farmer as he gradually turns his family farm into an industrial animal factory before realizing his mistakes and choosing a more sustainable path. The film gained over 300 million earned media impressions.[27]

Following the successful deliveries of those and similar campaigns, it was not long before countless numbers of brands began experimenting with building *experiences*.[28] Almost overnight, all brands felt the urge to tell stories, creating content that mimicked entertainment, integrating products into scripted and nonscripted TV, and exploring the opening world of engagement and interaction with offline and online communities.

Rising to be a storyteller

We have all the data in the world to support that content consumption is up on every device, every demographic, every region in the world. Every human who has access to a device is watching more content on it with each successive year. But at the same time, ad avoidance is also up on every device, every demographic, every region. So, if we're consuming more content than ever, but we're avoiding advertising at higher rates than ever, then the upper funnel is broken.[29] Like, so, if you can't create more of a thing that's being avoided more, you have to create more of what's actually being consumed. So, the market dynamic alone is what forces all marketers to have to seriously consider creating content that attracts and engages an audience rather than interrupts it.

—Jae Goodman, Observatory

In 2015, at one of the advertising industry's award festivals, there was a panel discussion about branded content. During questions from the audience, one person stood up and asked why, if every branded content campaign involves experts in the field, is there so much bad content coming from brands? It is a very fair question. Part of the answer may be that branded content is a relatively young genre and that means it is marked by a lot of trial and error; there are bound to be growing pains. In fact, the first branded content project of the modern advertising era dates only to 2001: BMW's short movie series directed by Guy Richie, *The Hire*. There is more to it, requiring in-depth inquiry into the industry's approach to entertainment content delivery.

Branded entertainment is "a communication effort that employs a compelling authentic narrative to achieve brand resonance".[30] It should be compelling enough that consumers would be ready to pay for the content with their time or money. As such, it can be inclusive of numerous forms and formats: short videos, integration of product messages into original programming, magazines, radio broadcasts, movies, music and gaming industry tie-ins, advertising-funded programing, and many more.[31] Because its inherent narrative properties aim to establish a strong emotional connection with a target audience and thus evoke consumer engagement, branded entertainment is considered one of the more compelling brand communication tools that can meaningfully contribute to brand narrative.[32]

Along with the increasing issues of reaching and grabbing the attention of audiences, there has been a corresponding increase in branded content and entertainment-centered campaigns. Countless brands have embraced the strategy, seeing it as a way to connect with consumers on a more personal level. However, as with any early period of broad acceptance, various critiques arose. The most prevalent ones fall at two nonexclusive poles—first, branded content and entertainment are newfangled concepts cooked up by digital marketers, who apply them without regard for broader marketing strategies or brand goals; second, branded content lacks actual value for consumers and people will reject overtly commercial content.[33] Some, like DentsuACHTUNG!'s founder and creative director, Mervyn Ten Dam, would go as far as calling out brands for recklessness in following the trend. He points out that maybe not all products should actually try to entertain us, especially if their role in consumers' lives is strictly functional.

The problem often seems to be rooted in a general misconception that brands see stories as an inherently successful form. "The market dynamic demands that all brands at this point need to create content that attracts and engages rather than just interrupt. They must do it in a way that's authentic to their brand and business[es] just can't just tell some random story and hope for the best", explains Jae Goodma, (ex-)CEO of Observatory Agency. This relates to the larger problem that businesses start out having all the wrong motivations to begin with—they do not want to have a more engaging dialogue with consumers by offering them the content they desire, but rather they are driven by the fear that traditional advertising is obsolete.[34] As Scott Dontaton pointed out already in 2002:

> Marketers are hot on the idea of product placement. . . . They've convinced themselves that giving it a new name (product integration) qualifies it as a creative concept rather than a recycled device from TV's earliest days. . . . Something is missing from the equation in the new marketing math: the consumer.[35]

The disconnection from audiences can be linked to the fact that increasingly savvy consumers can easily sense the content's inauthenticity as just another promo in different wrappings. This, in turn, can be linked with the brands' general approach to content development—a creative process—which, in most cases, does not differ much from traditional advertising. As Goodman points out:

> Products and brands act differently in entertainment. While on the brand side there is a temptation to "overbrand", which is driven by a desire to get maximum exposure for the product, the subtlety is key. Pushing the brand or product too much can take viewers out of the story, and it is not only something that Cannes judges are often quick to point out when a client is "showing" too much, but it's something that anyone who watches can see.

At the same time, it is important to note that branded entertainment as a strategy does not seem to be doomed to failure, as there are brands (or rather agencies and creatives) that manage to overcome the creative tensions that come with the advertising-entertainment content convergence. However, those who mastered brand entertainment as a new kind of genre tend to approach the creative process in a vastly different way than traditional advertising.

Learning from Hollywood

"If agencies want to succeed at branded entertainment, they need to think more like the competition. And, no I'm not talking about other agencies. I'm talking about Hollywood," urged Michael Wiese in 2010.

When we think about advertising formats as media genres, a 30-second TV ad is a very different medium than for-entertainment genres, such as sitcoms or documentaries. Therefore, it should not come as a surprise that they need different sets of skills. Even though the short stories offered within 30 seconds can be compelling and entertaining in their own right, the format does not offer much space for subtlety or slowly unfolding narratives. Its primary purpose is to deliver a product or brand message, distinguish the brand from others, and sell. Ad writers, thus, need to master the skill of distilling the "essence" of a pitch. Advertising professionals who manage to deliver successful branded entertainment projects (where success is defined as a combination of commercial success and audience satisfaction) share the opinion that quality branded entertainment is hard to deliver within traditional advertising models and processes, and call for a different approach. Crafting TV ads is a unique and specific expertise, and there is a clear indication that creatives who usually deliver ads in the traditional 30-second format cannot necessarily conceptualize, write, and direct longer entertainment forms.

The *5B* project introduced in the opening of this book is a full-length documentary, directed by Oscar nominee Dan Krauss and Oscar winner Paul Haggis, which tells the story of the first dedicated HIV ward but is also a prime example of brand-sponsored content that followed a Hollywood production protocol. The movie premiered in the main selection of the Cannes Film Festival in 2019 and is one of the very few films holding a 100% rating on the Rotten Tomatoes rating platform. Yet, no matter how good the production was, or how uplifting the heroic acts of the nurses were, the bittersweet history centering on true stories of death, fear, and social ostracism is not a natural environment for a brand presence. Indeed, no brand is visible or mentioned in the opening credits, nor in any of the 94-minute run-time. That the movie was central to a Johnson & Johnson campaign is unique in the advertising scene, in the sense that it was brand-initiated and brand-sponsored, but there is no direct or implicit link to the brand present in the production. Yet, the brand considered it effective and majorly successful. On the social cause level, the film was linked to the broader brand's mission—it was a strategic move aimed at building a stronger emotional connection with stakeholders from the medical sector, which is key for the brand's business. As Sarah Colamarino, then Vice President of Corporate Equity at Johnson & Johnson, explained in Saville Productions Purpose Podcast:

> We were at a critical moment, where we were transitioning the Johnson & Johnson brand for what most stakeholders knew, as a baby company, to really a health care company, and a health care company that really had the potential to change the trajectory of health. So that strategic fit was perfect, but it also fit with what the company had done for many years. It was a company for many years that has been dedicated to the recruitment, retention and development of nurses.[36]

Colamarino points out that the struggle of many marketers in delivering entertainment-based projects is a deeply rooted belief that the brand needs to be a hero, as they are used to thinking with traditional advertising:

> It's an opportunity, but it's a challenge, where we're all used to making sure that our brand name is out there. First and foremost, you have to think really differently. When you do a piece of brand purpose film, you've got to think about giving rise to the issue. And then surrounding that film, once it's done with the kinds of messaging that are best for your brand.

Interestingly, the practitioners involved in the development and production of such cases repeatedly mention that what they do is not product placement or branded content/entertainment, as it is commonly classified. They rather label it *brand purpose film*, *brand sponsored entertainment,* or *brand entertainment*, depending on who you ask, to highlight the distinction. Even though it is arguably a simple semantic distinction, there is a clear purpose and meaning behind this divergence, which indicates a broader paradigm shift. Productions such as *5B* deconstruct branded content to the point of being as distant from traditional advertising as possible. It is "not advertising" as Serazio[37] labels guerilla marketing, not (only) in the sense of applying methods that fall outside the scope of traditional marketing strategies but by deliberately avoiding contexts in which it might be easily identified as a traditional form of marketing. Therefore, the nominal change from branded entertainment to brand entertainment, on the one hand, brings forward the fact that the content is intended to provide entertainment, and it is coming from a brand. Yet, at the same time, it aims to steer away from negative connotations that openly branded forms may bring.

However, the differences do not end at the semantic level. The key difference between typical brand-centered content and *brand entertainment* lies in the entire approach to the project and its development and production process, which follows the principals of Hollywood rather than traditional advertising. "In the ad world", Rupert Maconick, a founder and executive producer at Saville Productions, explains: "[in traditional advertising] you always want to sell an idea. That's what everyone does. We sell the model, and embrace the model, and then follow a film and TV process that have a development phase". He describes the difference based on the *5B* example: "we mined for a unique story. . . . We [Saville Productions] were like the journalist and a newspaper; the brand and the agency were like the editors of a newspaper". He continued:

> You find a great director because you found a great story. We want somebody who's very experienced with docs, we want somebody [who has] never done an ad if possible. We also recommend the director has some level of editorial control of final cut. [When the film is done] we help with distribution, we'll bring in a sales agent, we'll help get it into film festivals. And we'll bring in a documentary festival PR. . . . And people want to watch it.

The process that makes a difference

Maconick is not alone in seeing the need for advertisers to behave more like Hollywood producers. Numerous experts operating within the blurred lines of advertising and entertainment suggest that marketers should take cues from native entertainment creators because they see value in entertainment-world practices and management of creative processes, which can help to advertise both by making brands' messages more visible and appealing to audiences and by helping the advertising industry improve its creative culture. Even though this book does not aim to provide a "how to" guide, tracing how brand entertainment practitioners perceive new practices unveils how advertising achieves this new syncretism.

Need for entertainment strategy

As previously discussed, since audiences have become less tolerant of advertising and avoid watching commercial content with the use of ad-blocking software and ad-free streaming platforms, brands have become more interested in producing content that does not rely on interruption or intrusion. However, experts see the need for a fundamental change of thinking about how this can be achieved:

> As a brand you have a strategy for influencers and social media, that you didn't have that 15 years ago. You now need a strategy to reach people on streaming platforms in an effective way. Let's create things that people want to watch. And the streamers will want to buy them because the audience watches them. Every streamer has the same thing, they have film and TV.

Developing a brand entertainment strategy requires time, patience, and a different perception of how marketing results can be achieved since brand entertainment needs to be considered as contributing more to the marketing upper funnel than the instant results of performance marketing. Hence, if an advertiser is used to "buying views" or paying for "eyeballs" in broadcast—and getting compensated by TV stations when a spot does not perform as promised[38]—or paying for online engagement and performance, then they expect immediate and direct attribution.[39] Rather, they need to consider brand entertainment as a tool that delivers results and builds connections with consumers over time.

Story coming before media planning and dealmaking

In the last 20 years, media planning and buying by media agencies grew in importance in the advertising landscape. For years the backwater of the industry, media agencies now use financial leverage to influence the media system toward new ways of analyzing audiences and defining a successful campaign.[40] Along with that, they also take the initiative in planning campaigns, deciding what ad formats to use, and where and how ads should be placed. Pushing media domination over content-making, ad agencies therefore oftentimes match creative work with their planning. By not delimiting the format first (to e.g., 30-, 60-, or 90-second TV ad or 2-minute YouTube video), media agencies allow for the story to come first and then find the right tools to most effectively deliver the message to target audiences.

The same holds true for allowing the story to take the lead over the choice of talent—oftentimes influencers with millions of followers. As experts suggest, they may guarantee access to target audiences, but they do not always reflect the project's character. "Brands tend to start out thinking they can buy their way into talent, and that will be enough to make their content great. Sure, most stars have their price, but if they're not committed to the project beyond the paycheck, it will show in the work"[41] as Brendan Shields-Shimizu from The Observatory Agency explains. Therefore, as practitioners stress, it becomes imperative to attach names that have the ability to bring the actual story to life and connect with the audience to tell an authentic story.

Development process over "wow" effect

A majority of traditionally structured agencies cooperate with their clients on what we could call the "wow" effect. The model of cooperation is one where clients brief the agency, which then works in disconnection from the client until they return with a final set of recommendations (as discussed in Chapter 2). In this model, the client is on the sideline and not much involved in the initial ideation and development process. What the experts suggest, however, is the necessity of building mutual trust between agencies and clients for entertainment-based projects to succeed. The development process needs to reflect traditional TV or film development, with extensive research and multiple people involved in writing a story that will not only engage audiences but also match the client's needs. This requires collaboration, frequent meetings, additional resources, and "trusting the process" as the practitioners repeatedly expressed. As Maconick explained regarding the example of collaboration with Johnson & Johnson on the *5B* movie:

> In our story, we said, we need two months to do a deep dive with a team of about a dozen people, who were documentary researchers, essentially journalists, and we will hunt for a unique story that no one's ever heard of. It will tap into all of your marketing goals and all your brand purpose. It won't feel like an ad. We mined for a unique story; it has to be better than what's on Netflix, or they went by or Amazon or it has to be the top 1% of docs. We presented them ideas every week [so it could be discussed and evolve], which was all based around their [J&J's] marketing objectives and brand purpose. And after about a month, we found the true story.

The changing role of clients in advertising (as in more traditional ad products) corresponds with research on cocreative processes and innovation in creative

and design-intensive sectors. It becomes clear that increased client involvement is key to designing and implementing successful innovations and links
directly to greater opportunities for developing new products and solutions.[42]
Those who are heavily involved in the project development stages are more
likely to support the project during its financing and production phase as they
may see themselves as co-creators and co-owners of the project.[43] However,
it is important to mention that both service providers (in this case creative
agencies) and clients may want to manage the cocreation, but, in some cases,
less collaboration may actually boost the quality of the finished result.[44]
Therefore, for creative agencies, the management of client involvement can
become an important tool for improving the chance of greenlighting creative
and innovative projects.

Collaboration and partnership over competition

The traditional agency creative process is very competitive, with teams fight-
ing to come up with the winning idea and individuals or creative teams of
two—art director and copywriter—competing for credit. In contrast, consider
the creative process of a film studio: moviemaking usually takes hundreds of
people and many weigh in to shape the idea. Goodman explains the way they
work in Observatory Agency (which used to be a subsidiary of Creative Artists Agency, henceforth CAA):

> Our feeling was always that we would take a more 'writers room'
> approach. . . . Let's say you had 10 creatives working on something—five
> teams. The creative director's job would be to hear ideas from all five
> teams, and then pick one or two. So, you're automatically just wildly inef-
> ficient. . . . Everything was a competition of ideas. And so, the thought that
> we had going into CAA was let's operate more like entertainment. . . . So,
> the person who had the idea might not be the person who builds on the
> idea, might not be the person who writes up the idea, might not be the per-
> son who presents the idea, might not be the person who goes and finds the
> producer for the idea might not be in it, which is by the end of the project,
> you might have 25 people who touched it.

The writers' room that Goodman points out is a concept that originated in
Hollywood, where screenwriters work together to develop film or television
scripts.[45] It is a highly creative and highly collaborative place, where writers
often bounce ideas off each other and make all the major decisions about the
show—from storylines to character development—to come up with the best
possible scripts. As a structure that promotes a creative spirit and encourages
collaboration within teams, the writers' room is a model that may be seen
as an alternative to the traditional in-agency model. Some advertising agencies are looking to consider and adopt this model, according to Lionel Curt,

co-founder, and CEO of MNSTR, a French independent agency specializing in storytelling-centered brand work:

> I was in a cafe in Paris, and I've seen some [people], they were writing a story for an episode, and there were five around the table. And they were all getting the ideas, and somebody was expanding them. I think we should be more and more looking into entertainment differently, and the way they work, and the way they process. It is my ambition to work like this. And we will have common ownership of that, meaning that we can distribute, then generate revenue, but also act like an advertising.

While the traditional model of the creative team is still dominant in the industry, it is increasingly being supplanted by a more collaborative approach. As the landscape of advertising changes, so too does the way creativity within the industry is achieved, where, once creativity was seen as a more isolated discipline, in the sense that it relies on an individual's skills and talent. Today, it is increasingly seen as an essential component of effective team management. This shift has been driven by the need for greater collaboration and partnership between different (rapidly growing) disciplines and roles within advertising, as well as recognition of the importance of collaborating with other creative sectors. As a result, creativity is becoming integral to the process of management. This shift has potential implications for the way in which creative agencies operate, with a greater emphasis on creativity as a cocreative value.

Giving up control and ownership

Goodman shared an anecdote with me:

> You know, like there is this very old joke that every copywriter has [a] half-finished script, right? We were working on a major entertainment project for a major brand that has one of the best ad agencies in the world. And when we were meeting to talk about the entertainment project, the very well-known chief creative officer who had come up through the business as a copywriter stood up. And she said, well, I want to write the movie, and the client for this mega brand then said: "Well, I understand that, we understand that, but we're going to have an Academy Award winning screenwriter write the screenplay".

The advertising industry is one that has long been based on the individual's creative genius. The idea of the lone artist and two-people partnerships, working in a frenzy of inspiration to create something meaningful, is one that popular culture has perpetuated for decades.[46] Even though collaborative approaches are increasingly common in creative agencies, for some creative, the idea of giving away (partial) creative control over the executed project is difficult to accept. Especially in the context of collaboration with external partners and talent, as Michael Wiese, who made a transition from an advertising agency to a broadcaster's in-house branded content studio, explains:

> I think one of the faults of creative EDs [executive directors] of ad agencies is they live in the world of client and vendor. And they "own" the client, they have full control of entire process, and then everyone's a vendor to them to serve the client. And in the entertainment business, everything's about partnership and collaboration.

As a result of the agencies' deeply ingrained need for creative control over what is presented to the client, collaborations and cocreation with stakeholders from other sectors may also be impacted. Maconick highlights the need for "letting it go" and trusting in the abilities of external teams that navigate and lead projects that require skills and expertise distant from those needed in advertising:

> None of us works our best when we're being micromanaged. If you've got someone looking over your shoulder making annoying comments, it doesn't help it actually. Once you've agreed on doing something, delegate and embrace the fact that you've brought in the right people and do it right, and then you're probably gonna be more successful.

In other words, putting too much pressure on an external team to comply with an agency's expectations and interfering with their internal process may negatively affect the outcome. What is interesting, this sentiment is echoed by agencies in their relations with clients. The previous research on agency–client relationships highlights a need for a clear brief[47] as a starting point for building mutual understanding but also for building trust, which will allow agencies to operate independently.[48] This dynamic exposes the complexity of building effective collaborative models of creative processes; on the one hand, there is a need for building partnerships and closer cooperation between stakeholders, and on the other hand, there is an experienced need for freedom and space, so everyone can "do their jobs".

However, collaboration in advertising can pose difficulties not only on the talent-to-talent level but also in the context of the business landscape of the industry. Fragmentation is making it more difficult for agencies to delineate their areas of specialization and responsibility as the lines between advertising, branding, PR, and media are becoming very blurred and "everyone does everything". In such environments, it is not uncommon for a brand to collaborate with a few or even a dozen different entities. Even though more agencies are open to the idea of working with external companies to collaborate and exchange experiences, it is not easy for them to share "their business" as it decreases the profit margin and marginalizes their role in the eyes of the client. In effect, it puts into question the value they bring. To offer an example: if there is a production studio leading the development of a brand-sponsored documentary, the role of the creative agency may become vague and may be limited to being an intermediary between a studio/broadcaster/publisher and the brand. Then, the challenge links back to the issue of the traditional client–agency billing business models. Where an agency could charge a client for the talent's hourly fees for 100 hours of TV spot development, now, their role may be limited to referring clients to an entertainment production company that operates on commission. As Wiese reflected: "In this sense, I am their nemesis or competitor [in his role in Disney's internal agency]. But at the same time, I know we need each other. There's no competition. It's like, we all got to work together".

Taking risks and having always pipeline of projects in development

On the topic of risk-taking, Maconick advises:

> The whole entertainment business is like: "your one hit pays for your 1010 flops." If you're a studio, that's true. You have to have those hits, but you need to take risks, you need to be bold, make big bets. And brands and advertisers need to think that way. It's like the Super Bowl, the biggest moment in advertising. It's like, this the best creative or this is the biggest idea or the most exciting commercial work going on. And those are also the biggest bets that brands are making. You can't build your whole business on that. You need a portfolio, but I think risk taking.

The Hollywood industry's knack for taking risks and diversifying its investments follows key factors that professionals suggest advertising agencies should emulate. This not only entails making braver recommendations to clients and encouraging them to take risks when it comes to their creative choices and campaign budgets but also includes having a pipeline of projects in development. While advertising agencies feel pressure to produce results quickly and on a tight budget, bringing well-developed new ideas to complex campaigns (especially long-form or event-driven content) is not possible in the current model, in which clients demand ideas to be delivered almost overnight. Similarly, to how Korsten discussed encouraging his creative teams to always have projects in development (as discussed in Chapter 2), entertainment professionals suggest that agencies should invest their own resources to work on the projects that they believe in and offer them to clients as more well-round ideas.

Despite the fact that agencies may complain that the customers resist taking risks and reject innovative work, research by Calderwood, Koslow, and Sasser demonstrates that competent agencies encourage risk-averse clients to take on work that is more creative.[49] They argue that clients who engage with competent agencies tend to purchase more creative ideas, as do clients who are willing to take risks. However, risk-averse clients who partner with less capable agencies receive less creative work.

Notes

1 Michael Wiese, SVP, Branded Content, National Geographic Partners & Head of Nat Geo CreativeWorks.
2 Boller, G. W., & Olson, J. (1991). Experiencing ad meaning: Crucial aspects of narrative/drama processing. In R. H. Holman & M. R. Solomon (Eds.), *Advances in consumer research* (Vol. 18, pp. 172–175). Association for Consumer Research.
3 Mattila, A. S. (2000). The role of narratives in the advertising of experiential services. *Journal of Service Research*, *3*(1), 35–45. https://doi.org/10.1177/109467050031003; Padgett, D., & Allen, D. (1997). Communicating experiences: A narrative approach to creating service brand image. *Journal of Advertising*, *26*(4), 49–62. https://doi.org/10.1080/00913367.1997.10673535.
4 Chang, C. (2009). "Being hooked" by editorial content: The implications for processing narrative advertising. *Journal of Advertising*, *38*(1), 21–34. https://doi.org/10.2753/joa0091-3367380102; Edson Escalas, J., Chapman Moore, M., & Edell Britton, J. (2004). Fishing for feelings? hooking viewers helps! *Journal of Consumer Psychology*, *14*(1–2), 105–114. https://doi.org/10.1207/s15327663jcp1401&2_12; Kang, J. A., Hong, S., & Hubbard, G. T. (2020). The role of storytelling in advertising: Consumer Emotion, narrative engagement level, and word-of-mouth intention. *Journal of Consumer Behaviour*, *19*(1), 47–56. https://doi.org/10.1002/cb.1793.
5 Edson Escalas, J. (1998). Advertising narratives. What are they and how do they work? In B. B. Stern (Ed.), *Representing consumers: Voices, views, and visions*. Routledge.
6 Rose, F. (2012). *The art of immersion: How the digital generation is remaking Hollywood, Madison Avenue, and the way we tell stories*. W. W. Norton & Company.
7 The typical American watched more than four hours of television every day in the late 1990s, according to the A.C. Nielsen Co. Most Western European countries reached 4 fours in early 2000s.
8 Reeves, R. (1990). *Reality in advertising*. Knopf.
9 Ibid; Rose, F. (2012). *The art of immersion: How the digital generation is remaking Hollywood, Madison Avenue, and the way we tell stories*. W. W. Norton & Company.
10 Donaton, S. (2005). *Madison & Vine: Why the entertainment and advertising industries must converge to survive*. McGraw-Hill.
11 Wasserman, T. (2020, August 10). The 30-second TV ad is history. Now what? *Forbes*. Retrieved September 21, 2022, from www.forbes.com/sites/toddwasserman/2020/08/10/the-30-second-tv-ad-is-history-now-what/?sh=180a23c62b1e.
12 Rose, F. (2012). *The art of immersion: How the digital generation is remaking Hollywood, Madison Avenue, and the way we tell stories*. W. W. Norton & Company.
13 Hudson, S., & Hudson, D. (2006). Branded entertainment: A new advertising technique or product placement in disguise? *Journal of Marketing Management*, *22*(5–6), 489–504. https://doi.org/10.1362/026725706777978703.
14 Elliott S. (2006, April 17). Advertisers now want to be directors, too. *New York Times*. http://www.iht.com/articles/2006/04/17/business/brand.php.
15 Hudson, S., & Hudson, D. (2006). Branded entertainment: A new advertising technique or product placement in disguise? *Journal of Marketing Management*, *22*(5–6), 489–504. https://doi.org/10.1362/026725706777978703.

16 Derda, I. (2018). A potted history of content in modern electronic media. In D. Lazar & J. Kirby (Eds.), *The definitive guide to strategic content marketing perspectives, issues, challenges and solutions* (pp. 113–115). Kogan Page Ltd.; Kretchmer, S. B. (2004). Advertainment: The evolution of product placement as a mass media marketing strategy. *Journal of Promotion Management*, *10*(1–2), 37–54. https://doi.org/10.1300/j057v10n01_04.

17 IMDb. (2014, September 7). Brändärit. *IMDb*. Retrieved September 21, 2022, from www.imdb.com/title/tt3918460/.

18 Eurobest. (2014). 2014 branded content & entertainment. *Eurobest*. Retrieved September 21, 2022, from https://www2.eurobest.com/winners/2014/branded/.

19 Personal communication (2014).

20 Havrilesky, H. (2014, February 28). The brilliant, unnerving meta-marketing of 'the Lego movie'. *The New York Times*. Retrieved September 21, 2022, from www.nytimes.com/2014/03/02/magazine/the-brilliant-unnerving-meta-marketing-of-the-lego-movie.html.

21 Smithson, P. (2014, April 17). The Lego movie: Content marketing at its finest. *The Guardian*. Retrieved September 21, 2022, from www.theguardian.com/media-network/media-network-blog/2014/apr/17/lego-movie-content-marketing.

22 IMDb. (2014, February 7). The Lego movie. *IMDb*. Retrieved September 21, 2022, from www.imdb.com/title/tt1490017/?ref_=fn_al_tt_1.

23 The LEGO Group. (2015). The Lego Group annual report 2014. *Lego.com*. Retrieved September 21, 2022, from www.lego.com/cdn/cs/aboutus/assets/blta425337e673c7461/Annual_Report_2014_ENG.pdf.

24 The LEGO Group. (2016). The Lego Group annual report 2015. *Lego.com*. Retrieved September 21, 2022, from www.lego.com/cdn/cs/aboutus/assets/blt7f153c705df8d024/Annual_Report_2015_ENG.pdf.

25 Stein, L. (2013). Dove's sketches campaign turns heads at Cannes. *PR Week*. Retrieved September 21, 2022, from www.prweek.com/article/1275452/doves-sketches-campaign-turns-heads-cannes.

26 Red Bull. (2012). Relive one of the moments of the decade: Red Bull Stratos. *Red Bull*. Retrieved September 21, 2022, from www.redbull.com/int-en/best-of-2012-red-bull-stratos.

27 Observatory Agency. (2013). Chipotle: Back to the start. *Observatory Agency*. Retrieved September 21, 2022, from https://observatoryagency.com/work/back-to-the-start.

28 Rose, F. (2012). *The art of immersion: How the digital generation is remaking Hollywood, Madison Avenue, and the way we tell stories*. W. W. Norton & Company.

29 Goodman refers here to the marketing upper funnel, which is an approach that considers the initial awareness stage of a consumer's journey. Heinz, M. (2016). *Full funnel marketing: How to embrace revenue responsibility and increase marketing's influence on pipeline growth and closed deals*. Heinz Marketing Press.

30 van Loggerenberg, M. J. C., Enslin, C., & Terblanche-Smit, M. (2019). Towards a definition for branded entertainment: An exploratory study. *Journal of Marketing Communications*, *27*(3), 322–342. https://doi.org/10.1080/13527266.2019.1643395.

31 Donaton, S. (2005). *Madison & Vine: Why the entertainment and advertising industries must converge to survive*. McGraw-Hill.

32 Dahlén, M., Lange, F., & Smith, T. (2010). *Marketing communications: A brand narrative approach*. Wiley.

33 Donaton, S. (2005). *Madison & Vine: Why the entertainment and advertising industries must converge to survive*. McGraw-Hill.

34 Ibid.

35 Ibid.

36 Maconick, R. (2022). Sarah Colamarino on the documentary 5B. *Saville Productions Purpose Podcast*. Retrieved September 21, 2022, from https://podcasts.apple.com/us/podcast/sarah-colamarino-on-the-documentary-5b/id1608231235?i=1000550600053.

37 Serazio, M. (2013). *Your ad here: The cool sell of guerrilla marketing*. New York University Press.

38 In such cases, the advertiser can be offered a spot on a comparable schedule. This may include moving the program to another time in the schedule or placing a spot next to another program within the same daypart. (Katz, H. E. (2022). *The media handbook: A complete guide to advertising media selection, planning, research, and buying*. Routledge, Taylor & Francis Group).

39 Beer, J. (2022, July 15). Brands can make Hollywood-level entertainment. This guy proved it. *Fast Company*. Retrieved September 21, 2022, from www.fastcompany.com/90769767/brands-can-make-entertainment-as-good-as-hollywood-and-this-guy-proved-it.

40 Turow, J. (2011). *The daily you: How the new advertising industry is defining your identity and your worth*. Yale University Press.

41 Shields-Shimizu, B. (2022). What an 'MBA in entertainment' can teach us about brand content. *Muse by Clio*. Retrieved September 21, 2022, from https://musebycl.io/film-tv/what-mba-entertainment-can-teach-us-about-brand-content.

42 Kilinc, N., Ozturk, G. B., & Yitmen, I. (2015). The changing role of the client in driving innovation for design-build projects: Stakeholders' perspective. *Procedia Economics and Finance, 21*, 279–287. https://doi.org/10.1016/s2212-5671(15)00178-1.

43 Buur, J., & Matthews, B. (2008). Participatory innovation. *International Journal of Innovation Management, 12*(3), 255–273. https://doi.org/10.1142/s1363919608001996; Edvardsson, B., Gustafsson, A., Kristensson, P., Magnusson, P., & Matthing, J. (2010). *Involving customers in new service development*. ICP; Öberg, C. (2010). Customer roles in innovations. *International Journal of Innovation Management, 14*(6), 989–1011. https://doi.org/10.1142/s1363919610002970.

44 Lehrer, M., Ordanini, A., DeFillippi, R., & Miozzo, M. (2012). Challenging the orthodoxy of value co-creation theory: A contingent view of co-production in design-intensive business services. *European Management Journal, 30*(6), 499–509. https://doi.org/10.1016/j.emj.2012.07.006.

45 Karhula, M., Lehti, T., & Nuutinen, T. (2021). *The writers' room*. Metropolia University of Applied Sciences.

46 Bilton, C. (2011). Relocating creativity in advertising. In A. C. Pratt & P. Jeffcutt (Eds.), *Creativity, innovation and the cultural economy*. Routledge.

47 Blakeman, R. (2015). *Advertising campaign design: Just the essentials*. Routledge.

48 Kaats, E., & Opheij, W. (2014). *Creating conditions for promising collaboration alliances, networks, chains, strategic partnerships*. Springer.

49 Calderwood, R., Koslow, S., & Sasser, S. L. (2021). Marketer perceptions of client—agency co-creation: Exploring the levels of partnership collaboration. *Journal of Advertising, 50*(3), 309–319. https://doi.org/10.1080/00913367.2020.1868027.

4 Advertising X other creative sectors

Art and advertising have a long and intertwined history and are not as distinct from each other as they may initially seem. Even though the apparent difference between them lies in the fact that ads are about selling pieces of the world, whereas art is about showing its beauty and ugliness,[1] they are closely interrelated on few levels.[2] Advertisements are at their core functional and are supposed to produce unambiguous behavioral outcomes (such as persuading, pursuing information, and boosting sales), while works of art may be deliberately polysemic in order to facilitate the creation of diverse interpretations among the audience.[3] Advertising utilizes artistic accomplishments in color, finesse, and abstraction to convey its commercial message,[4] and from the opposite direction, art employs components taken from advertising, often to criticize modern consumerism, as in the work of Andy Warhol and Barbara Kruger.[5] Similar to how numerous art critics argue that "truly great art" is open-ended,[6] more than two-thirds of advertising experts agree that "the finest advertisements . . . leave something to the viewer's imagination" as Young explained.[7] Others, such as Hetsroni and Tukachinsky, go as far as suggesting that, in some circumstances, the only factor separating "pure" arts from ads is their setting: an art gallery versus an advertising channel.[8] In other instances, we can find adverts displayed in museums[9] or experience exhibitions built around and sponsored by specific brands, like the fashion exhibitions *Giorgio Armani* at the Guggenheim Museum[10] or *Vivienne Westwood* at the Victoria and Albert Museum[11] (though these are not without their controversies).[12]

As much as advertising has long included visual and contextual references to works of art in order to create a more lasting impression on viewers,[13] it has also established extensive relationships with all cultural and creative sectors. For example, advertising contributes to the development of other promotional genres of media, from music videos[14] to fashion films.[15] Rooted in the mass marketing of popular songs and luxury fashion, the hybrids of audiovisual advertisements with film and video art apply the persuasive logic of branded content[16] and follow the principles of experiential marketing to provide "sensory, emotional, cognitive, and relational values".[17]

DOI: 10.4324/9781003263128-5

At the same time, as ads evolve into new forms along with the changing media landscape, similar to the entertainment-based hybrids discussed in a previous chapter, industry professionals utilize the techniques of various creative sectors to deconstruct advertisements, conceal their persuasive nature, and appeal to audiences. Take, for example, an advertisement for the series *Money Heist*, a Spanish crime drama, which took a form of a sculpture. Located in the high-traffic location in the Old Town of Cracow, it shows the characteristic mustache mask that appears in the series, resembling the face of Salvador Dali. The mask stood right next to (almost mocking) the sculpture *Eros Bendato* by Igor Mitoraj, an artist renowned for his fragmented sculptures of the human body, frequently made for sizable public installations. Netflix's sculpture is accompanied by the inscription "Theft is real art". Like guerilla marketing that meets audiences in unexpected places (as demanded by Serazio)[18] and "steals" their attention, this advert demonstrates that "the medium is the message".[19] The work relies on the elements of unexpectedness and sensationalism to draw attention and drive curiosity,[20] and plays with the audience's ability to recognize the symbolism of the mask, decode the message, and link it properly with a TV show—contributing to the feeling of accomplishment for those who manage to do so. But the brands' motivations seem to exceed the need for unexpectedness and sensationalism. Patricia Aufderheide, states:

> It is easy to see why commercials have imitated music videos. . .
> It is not merely that advertisers like the pleasure-happy attitude that the [music] videos promote . . . It is also that music video never delivers a hard sell . . . Instead, it equates the product with an experience to be shared, part of a wondrous leisure world.[21]

However, tapping into consumers' desire for leisure and escapism to deliver an overall pleasurable experience is only one side of the coin. Engagement with various creative industries allows brands to tap into cultural trends, link to social issues, and build a more authentic voice in communication with their target audiences. Hence, this chapter looks beyond how creatives borrow tools and aesthetics from the arts world and follows two notions that become significant aspects of exchange occurring between advertising and other creative sectors. It follows how advertising takes advantage of the cultural and social potential of cultural production for tapping into current societal problems and connecting with specific targets to build more authentic narratives (that can attract both audiences and talent). Simultaneously, even though it clearly does not exhaust the breadth and depth of the practices of exchange, the discussion builds on the selected examples of advertising interacting with the arts to explore how various creative regimes inevitably clash with each other, leading to conflicts and tensions in cocreative processes.

Taking a stand

On June 9, 2018, a few hours before the start of festivities for the Equality Parade in Warsaw, Poland, a water-light hologram was illuminated in the colors of the rainbow flag. The symbol of equal rights and love appeared on Zbawiciela Square, a hip, central Warsaw location known for being a gathering place for the capital's liberal and artsy crowd. The scene was a recreation of an art installation by Julita Wójcik: a rainbow originally made of multicolored flowers, which first appeared in Wigry to support the walls of the local Camaldolese monastery. Later, it was presented in Brussels, in the square in front of the European Parliament, as part of the "Fossils and Gardens" art installation, on the occasion of the Polish presidency in the European Union. Finally, it landed in Warsaw in 2012 and ever since has functioned as a symbol of LGBT pride. As such, it became an object of merciless attacks by football hooligans and neo-fascist circles for whom the rainbow read as a "faggot rainbow" and, in consequence, was burned down seven times in three years and rebuilt with the involvement of the public. The return of the Rainbow in 2018 was initiated by Ben & Jerry's, the ice cream brand, in collaboration with the Love Does Not Exclude Association and Volunteers of Equality Foundation, so that it could no longer be destroyed. It was intended to raise awareness of the violation of LGBT rights in Poland.

Interestingly, the original art piece was not meant to be symbolic of LGBT equality but was intended to be politics-free. As the artist herself explained:

> Rainbow appeared at the time of organizing many events: on June 2, 2012, the Equality Parade took place, in a moment we will have Corpus Christi, and then the opening of Euro 2012. It fits in some way with all these events, which makes it emphasize my main assumption: that "Rainbow" should not be socially or politically engaged, that it would be completely free from any imposed meanings. Simply put—to be beautiful.[22]

Even though cause engagement was not the original purpose of the art installation, it grew to be a symbol of the fight for equality in the eyes of society or, as Wójcik herself once called the Rainbow, a litmus test, perfectly measuring social mood in Poland,[23] and the brand attached itself to this acquired symbolism. The artist gave permission to commercial activation, making her artwork an indirectly branded advertising medium for its sponsor.

In the wave of hip consumerism, which has emerged in opposition to traditional "mindless" consumerism (consumption for consumption's sake),[24] equality movements are increasingly represented through brands acting as saviors in the name of equality.[25] "Woke" marketing by Ben & Jerry's is not an isolated case but rather a major trend in advertising with brands tapping into all kinds of social issues. With as many as 70% of customers[26] feeling that brands should take a public stance on social and political issues and 66% who trust that brands can effect meaningful change,[27] businesses are recognizing the necessity to adjust their marketing tactics in a hyperpolitically aware brand environment. The notion is clearly apparent in the 2022 Cannes Festival winners, with 28 of 32 of the Grand Prix winning campaigns focusing on accessibility, gender equity, public health, climate change, and political activism.[28] Tapping into current social issues is a marketing strategy driven by both opportunism and necessity, as VMLY&R's Dawid Szczepaniak explains:

> It is now evident that this is the easiest way to create a campaign that stands out, paradoxically. The world is in the situation it is, and this is the answer to what is happening. This is fully justified; it is impossible to pretend that everything around us is fine, and brands have to react to it.

One outstanding practice is commodity activism, a consolidation of political and social objectives with consumer behavior where activism is achieved through branded capitalist frames. This means that individuals utilize brand consumption to express their identity politics.[29] As politics becomes more personal, crowd cultures collide, and "hip consumerism" emerges.[30] Hence, brands can take a political stand beyond just "posturing" or "virtue signaling", by attempting to grow revenue and tap into new markets by pandering to the social conscience of consumers.[31] At the same time, brands keep receiving criticism for using social justice and eco rhetoric for commercial gain. When done poorly, such messaging appears insincere and merits accusations of "woke-washing" and "tokenism".[32] This can be seen as symptomatic of the advertising industry:

> I worry about a growing trend of companies and agencies—even those not directly responsible for global climate change—chasing the shiny advertising object of "purpose" without committing to concrete action. This is dangerous for consumers and for the global good. If that's not argument enough, it also positions advertising professionals and agencies as untrustworthy messengers. We cannot allow ourselves to become the industry that cried "purpose,"[33]

warns Amelia Penniman, a strategic communications director at Bully Pulpit Interactive. Some, like Szczepaniak, raise the point of the potential fatigue of engaged marketing:

> This is where the turning point will finally come. It is inevitable that it must sooner or later trigger some kind of reaction that brands and people will be so tired of the whole mass of campaigns that help in a shallow, insincere way. Sooner or later, it will make the recipients tired, and we will return to campaigns that are clever, humorous, and perhaps without this aspect of saving the world.

Even though Ben & Jerry's has a long history of supporting causes that are important to its employees and leaders through its philosophy of "activism-infused capitalism",[34] such aspirational authenticity and "realness initiatives" often appear as sugar-coated attempts to include the audiences in a consumerist cultural matrix.[35] Brands like the ice cream producer, therefore, attempt to partner with other creative sectors that can help them come across as sincere in their attempt to build authenticity. "Brands do this, because it's *the easiest.* It takes years to build authenticity in social causes engagement. It takes tons of consistency and efforts. And brands use the fact that an artist is a real voice on the topic; and such collaboration gives [the] brand a platform to talk, more importantly gives them [the] RIGHT to talk", says an executive creative director, who asked for anonymity.

Embedding in culture

Collaborations between artists and brands can elevate the latter to iconic status and help them to become the embodiment of significant symbolic representations for individuals. Previous studies have shown that the more symbolic a brand is, the better it is perceived. This is because symbolic brands are seen as embodying significant cultural representations that resonate with consumers.[36] Street art, understood as an urban form of expression that includes tagging, graffiti, murals, stenciling, wheat pasting, stickers, freehand drawing, and a variety of other street installations,[37] is one such artistic practice that has a long association with youth culture and the expression of a community's social and economic ideals.[38] Originally occurring in public areas without the permission of property owners (although there is an increasing number of commissioned works), street art is understood as an illicit activity and is, by definition, a subversive art.[39] Yet, it is also particularly connected with the rehabilitation of communities and cities, which is frequently accomplished through community arts collaborations[40] and has been proven to help repair a city's reputation after a period of violence.[41] The approach of seeing the street art as a tool for community building and cohesion in times of crisis[42] was also visible during the Covid-19 pandemic. Responding to the aftermath of the series of lockdowns, which led many people to feel overwhelmed with negativity, anxiety, and feelings of isolation, some saw street art as a tool that could play an important role in fostering a sense of community and connection by allowing people to appreciate (branded) art in public places.[43] As John Flaherty, managing director of Mural Republic, and James Byard, head of Active Kinetic Worldwide, state: "The explosion and dominance of Coronavirus news alongside an increased focus on the negative elements and content on social media platforms have increased the relative value of more positive media environments like murals".[44]

Even though many street artists feel their work should not be a "tradeable commodity", as it is an artistic practice with subcultural content that thrives and spreads within a neoliberal environment, to characterize street art as exclusively antimainstream or antimarketing would be a mistake, as Damien Droney points out.[45] While claiming to reject the effects of consumerist culture, numerous street artists (ironically) cooperate with corporate marketing.[46] Many businesses attempt to use street art as a selling strategy,[47] seeing it as a tool that can help brands communicate with younger customers and develop an "authentic voice". However, the approach supports brands not only via participation and acknowledgment but also by enhancing the brand experience through community bonding, establishing an impression of authenticity, "coolness", and socially propagating the brand. As Flaherty and Byard continue:

> Murals offer brands an opportunity to embed themselves into the fabric of a community and engage their audiences in a highly creative way, on a grand scale, and with a degree of permanence. This handcrafted media has shown that advertising can transcend its own message and connect with people on a more human level.[48]

By adopting the aesthetics of authority and using "self-referential, ironic, meta-marketing",[49] creative agencies get an opportunity to reach a more sophisticated crowd that is skeptical of traditional marketing techniques and suspicious of contrived attempts at marketing.

By applying the strategy to embed itself in the social environments of consumers, global brands have been big (financial) supporters of street art movements, either directly with artists or through sponsorship.[50] By doing so, they elevate the status of some artists to successful entrepreneurs.[51] However, as street artists appropriating advertising and marketers employing subversive tactics converge, tension arises between the subversion of traditional aesthetic values and the reinforcement of capitalist ideologies. Advertising perpetuates the status quo by appearing to be a reflection of social reality.[52] Thus, while street art may initially appear to subvert the hegemony of mainstream culture, it can also inadvertently reinforce dominant ideologies by serving as a marketing tool.[53] There is a growing trend of marketers and artists alike who are playing with the categories that traditionally define their artistic practice and, thus, find mutual interest in creating ironic overlaps between the two seemingly antagonistic vocations of arts and (deconstructed) advertising.

Searching for "cool"

For the advertising industry and creative agencies, specifically, engagement with other creative sectors is much sought after and has more far-reaching implications as the industry struggles to attract young talent.

> We are not cool anymore. We do not create things that are culturally important [for young people], such as entertainment, gaming, e-sport, NGOs,

start-ups. These are the industries we compete with [for employees]. It used to be an ethos—if someone wanted to be cool, they went to work in the advertising industry. [Now] The ethos of success for young, talented people is elsewhere . . . So, we must try to give young people the opportunity to work on topics that interest them and are close to them.

As Szczepaniak explains, cross-sectoral collaborations can help advertising reposition itself in the eyes of the youth. Solitaire Townsend, a co-founder at the purpose-focused agency Futerra, echoes linking to purpose-oriented marketing: "All the young people that come to work for me want to work in a way that's in line with their values", she explains. "They don't want to use all their talent, all their ideas, all their creativity, all their ideation, on briefs that they don't think are making the world a better place".[54] This situation finds its reflection in the approach taken by some creative agencies' leaders to earning new clients or executing projects, according to a Milan-based agency managing director:

This is a reason why we want to win some clients so badly sometimes. There are those brands that are not always very profitable for us, but we all are just very excited to work for. There are brands that mean for us things like organizing concerts, gaming events, celeb meet-ups, things we would want take part in.

The focus on intersectoral engagement can be understood as a response to the industry's struggle to attract young talent and a tool for driving in-agency engagement since cooperatives whose members are drawn from different industries offer the potential to be more socially advantageous than those occurring within the same sector.[55] Involvement in diverse industries additionally allows for fresh perspectives and innovative approaches to solve clients' problems, as in the case of the Next Rembrandt, which utilized cooperation between various industries to enhance the creative and technical abilities possessed by the agency. Previous academic research supports the idea that intersector collaboration can lead to enhanced creativity and innovation within organizations. For example, a study by Geert Steurs[56] found that inter-industry R&D spillovers significantly affect a company's incentives to engage in innovation projects, both directly and indirectly. Those with high levels of interindustry collaboration exhibited higher levels of innovation. Therefore, embracing cross-sector engagement is not simply a means of attracting young talent but also a key strategic decision with the potential to drive growth, creativity, and innovation in creative agencies.

As we talk about "coolness", some may consider it to be an exaggerated narrative, in the context of the advertising industry. One the one hand, it relates to the freedom, informality, and glamour that are often associated with work in advertising agencies.[57] On the other hand, however, combined with the macho-workaholic environments of many agencies, "coolness" leads to the "social splitting" of creative workers, who are challenged to juggle the actual work conditions with the broader social implications of being cool.[58] A typical challenge for creative workers is that they are often caught in the middle—wanting to maintain the cool persona that distinguishes advertising from other white-collar workers[59]—but also needing to deal with challenging work conditions. This can be a difficult balance to maintain, and it can be especially challenging for those who are new to the industry. Hence, the issue that advertising may not be "cool enough" for young talent can be linked to the great resignation and the rejection of working environments that they perceive as exploitative in favor of a "higher purpose", as discussed in Chapter 1.

"Cool" carries with it a sense of detachment, an ability to remain unaffected by the mundane details of everyday life,[60] but it can also be a useful concept to understand today's advertising practices. As Douglas Holt points out, in a postmodern branding paradigm, for brands to be perceived as authentic, they need to act *disinterested*. They need to appear to have originated with parties without a financial motive, who are driven only by their intrinsic worth. Brands, therefore, are more valuable if they appear as cultural resources rather than cultural blueprints,[61] using strategies to hide persuasive communication in the form of cultural products.

Dealing with collaboration complexity

"I don't really do anything that's not within my visual style. I would not [agree to] work on something if the artwork was going to look like I didn't produce it. Because people who maybe know my work, would know that that mural was by me, they'd know certain elements that I always do, my visual style. If they [agency and client] came to a point where I couldn't tell that I did it, then that's where I'd be not interested in taking the project," Marcus Method, a UK-based visual artist known for his colorful signature style, explains his approach to commissioned projects.

The collaboration between advertising and other creative sectors is complex and differs from traditional creative processes of the ad world. This results from the general imperative of such partnerships that artists are not willing to allow themselves to be imposed upon, which is unlike advertising's culture of sticking to creative briefs and following brand strategies. Artists do take pride in producing work that bears their unique stamp, and as a result, some resist incorporating others' ideas into their projects. A common concern for artists is that "the input might contaminate or dilute the special quality that marks the work as their own".[62] As a German musician with experience composing for over a dozen major global brands elaborates (not without some irritation):

If they [a brand or an agency] come to me, I assume they know my music. And they came to me because of it. So, they want my interpretation of the topic they bring. So, I really don't understand all the talking and requests to the finished project. They want MY work, so they get MY work . . . Now I only work with brands that can get that.

On the other end, many creative agency representatives declare that they recognize that hiring artists means giving up control to some extent and that, in the world of the arts, very little can be achieved with a "manager knows best" mentality.[63] However, they also point out that an "I will not change anything" attitude, which they recognize in some artists, does not make them seem openminded or ready for cocreative work. As an executive creative director of a Scandinavian independent agency explains:

[We collaborate with artists] Because they have this unique style. Or because they can talk the audience "language". Which we not always can. It would be pointless to hire an artist like DJ, illustrator, indie designer and tell them what to do. That we can do it in-house. Our role is choosing right people for right projects. If we choose right, we should just let them do their job, eventually course-correct, if needed. . . . They need to know that we are in this together. . . . We are the ones who defend the thing in front of the client. We take the responsibility of what they do. We need to have A say.

Even though many agency leaders affirm openness, they can mistakenly interpret an artist's attitudes and actions as haughtiness rather than as expressions of creative identity[64] or differences in attitudes toward creative work and managerial styles. Such differences are deeply rooted in resistance toward capitalistic values and find expression in the topics of social justice, moral leadership, employee empowerment, and values that go beyond profit, which are frequently "off the radar" in an advertising agency setting[65] and in "critiques of top-down, quasi-scientific management practice".[66] Hence, it becomes apparent that cross-sectoral collaborations unveil the tension between artistic expression and commercialism. Artists may see a fundamental antagonism between their own goals and those of their employers, causing them to resist influence from colleagues that they perceive to be more profit-minded. This can lead to considerable tension within the workplace, as each side tries to assert its own priorities and requires much understanding to be developed on both ends.

Such collaborations can be also challenging for the creatives on the agency side, who do not receive ownership of the creative work (as discussed in previous chapters), and likewise for the agency managers, who must rethink each team member's role in the creative process and how it affects the dynamics of teamwork and creativity. That said, experts express that involving artists in an advertising project should not mean that the agency is completely hands-off, but rather that they work closely with the artists, offering feedback and suggestions where appropriate. As elaborated by Lionel Curt

> Sometimes the positioning in terms of agency is a bit strange, because you work with artists, and it's always that you did the work. . . . We manage the artists, we find the good artists that was matching with your [client's] problem [But] working with an artist doesn't mean that you let him do exactly what he wants. You also have to find the right balance to say 'okay, what we are doing here is this, and you're doing this, maybe we can go there. So it's a proper job [to manage a process].

However, it is also possible for this tension to result in a more creative and productive working environment, and the recent trend toward more cocreation among agencies and artists has not gone unnoticed. As Eric Haze, a street art pioneer, recognizes in pointing out some of the benefits of the brand—arts relationship:

> I think the trend or the market for collaborations, when it started in the late 90s, wasn't as collaborative as it is now. What started as sort of just holding hands has grown into a really, truly collaborative spirit. Where I'm not just functioning as a designer, but the brands sort of stand together in a new life because of the collaboration. You know, the essence of it is that we each bring something unique to the table. So, when the collaboration is right, each partner is receiving some new energy and identity from the other.[67]

As different perspectives come into dialogue with one another, ultimately, it is up to individual artists to decide how much they are willing to compromise in order to achieve success (understood as bringing a project to completion) and up to agencies to decide how much creative control they are ready to give up. "I actually like when they [artists] challenge our ideas. You know, we work with each other a lot, we know what kind of ideas can expect. We kind of live in our bubble. And then someone comes and says, 'you get it all wrong!' And it can be refreshing", reflects the London-based creative director of a network agency. Therefore, even though the power dynamics of arts–advertising collaborations can limit an artist's ability to exercise agency and make autonomous decisions about their work (which may compromise their artistic integrity and ultimately hinder the project's success), it seems possible to execute balance. Ultimately, it is crucial for artists to actively assert their agency in decision-making processes and strive for projects that align with their personal values and creative vision.

Obvious though it may seem, effective artist-agency cooperation requires both sides to develop more understanding of each other's perspectives and the nature of collaboration. For agency representatives, it is key to understand that collaborating artists might occasionally reject their ideas, and they should not impose their own vision on artists. On the contrary, they should offer suggestions that build on the artist's own ideas and provide advice that does not feel like a breach of the person's signature expression, holistic control, and noncommercial ethics.[68]

Notes

1 Varnedoe, K. (1991). Advertising. In A. Gopnik & K. Varnedoe (Eds.), *High and low: Modern art and popular culture* (pp. 231–368). Museum of Modern Art.
2 Ibid; Walker, J. (2020). *Art in the age of mass media*. Routledge.
3 Messaris, P. (2006). *Visual persuasion: The role of images in advertising*. Sage.
4 Walker, J. (2020). *Art in the age of mass media*. Routledge.
5 Varnedoe, K. (1991). Advertising. In A. Gopnik & K. Varnedoe (Eds.), *High and low: Modern art and popular culture* (pp. 231–368). Museum of Modern Art.
6 Kreitler, H., & Kreitler, S. (1978). *Psychology of the arts*. Duke University Press.
7 Young, C. E. (2000). Creative differences between copywriters and art directors. *Journal of Advertising Research, 40*(3), 19–26. https://doi.org/10.2501/jar-40-3-19-26.
8 Hetsroni, A., & Tukachinsky, R. H. (2005). The use of fine art in advertising: A survey of creatives and content analysis of advertisements. *Journal of Current Issues & Research in Advertising, 27*(1), 93–107. https://doi.org/10.1080/10641734.2005.10505176.
9 Ofrat, G. (1976). *Hagdarat ha-Omanut* [Hebrew: *The definition of art*]. Bari Press.
10 The Guggenheim Museums and Foundation. (2001). Giorgio Armani. *The Guggenheim Museums and Foundation*. Retrieved October 2, 2022, from www.guggenheim.org/exhibition/giorgio-armani
11 Victoria and Albert Museum. (2009). Vivienne Westwood. *Victoria and Albert Museum*. Retrieved October 2, 2022, from www.vam.ac.uk/collections/vivienne-westwood.
12 Steele, V. (2008). Museum quality: The rise of the fashion exhibition. *Fashion Theory, 12*(1), 7–30. https://doi.org/10.2752/175174108x268127.
13 Bogart, M. H. (1999). *Artists, advertising, and the borders of art*. University of Chicago Press.
14 Aufderheide, P. (1986). Music videos: The look of the sound. *Journal of Communication, 36*(1), 57–78. https://doi.org/10.1111/j.1460-2466.1986.tb03039.x.
15 Díaz Soloaga, P., & García Guerrero, L. (2016). Fashion films as a new communication format to build fashion brands. *Communication & Society, 29*(2), 45–61. https://doi.org/10.15581/003.29.2.45-61.
16 Del Pino Romero, C., & Castelló Martínez, A. (2015). La Comunicación Publicitaria Se Pone de Moda: Branded content y fashion films. *Revista Mediterránea De Comunicación, 6*(1), 105. https://doi.org/10.14198/medcom2015.6.1.07.
17 Atwal, G., & Williams, A. (2017). Luxury brand marketing—the experience is everything! *Advances in Luxury Brand Management*, 43–57. https://doi.org/10.1007/978-3-319-51127-6_3.
18 Serazio, M. (2013). *Your ad here: The cool sell of guerrilla marketing*. New York University Press.
19 McLuhan, M. (1969). *Understanding media: The extensions of man*. Sphere Books Limited.
20 Hutter, K., & Hoffmann, S. (2011). Guerrilla marketing: The nature of the concept and propositions for further research. *Asian Journal of Marketing, 5*(2), 39–54. https://doi.org/10.3923/ajm.2011.39.54.

21 Aufderheide, P. (1986). Music videos: The look of the sound. *Journal of Communication*, 36(1), 57–78. https://doi.org/10.1111/j.1460-2466.1986.tb03039.x

22 Culture.pl. (n.d.). Julita Wójcik, "Tęcza". *Culture.pl*. Retrieved October 5, 2022, from https://culture.pl/pl/dzielo/julita-wojcik-tecza.

23 Ibid.

24 Khamis, S. (2019). 'There's nothing wrong with the picture': Representations of diversity through cultural branding. *Media International Australia*, *172*(1), 89–102. https://doi.org/10.1177/1329878x19830820.

25 Jackson, S. J. (2016). (Re)imagining intersectional democracy from Black Feminism to hashtag activism. *Women's Studies in Communication*, *39*(4), 375–379. https://doi.org/10.1080/07491409.2016.1226654.

26 In the US.

27 Sprout Social. (2020, July 2). #brandsgetreal: Brands creating change in the conscious consumer era. *Sprout Social*. Retrieved October 5, 2022, from https://sproutsocial.com/insights/data/brands-creating-change/; Wertz, J. (2022, April 21). How social values drive consumers to brands. *Forbes*. Retrieved October 5, 2022, from www.forbes.com/sites/jiawertz/2021/12/27/how-social-values-drive-consumers-to-brands/?sh=5a3ce4737425.

28 Cannes Lions. (2022). Awards highlights. *Cannes Lions*. Retrieved October 5, 2022, from www.canneslions.com/enter/awards/awards-highlights.

29 Mukherjee, R., & Banet-Weiser, S. (2012). *Commodity activism: Cultural resistance in neoliberal times*. New York University Press.

30 Khamis, S. (2019). 'There's nothing wrong with the picture': Representations of diversity through cultural branding. *Media International Australia*, *172*(1), 89–102. https://doi.org/10.1177/1329878x19830820.

31 Mirzaei, A., Wilkie, D. C., & Siuki, H. (2022). Woke brand activism authenticity or the lack of it. *Journal of Business Research*, *139*, 1–12. https://doi.org/10.1016/j.jbusres.2021.09.044.

32 Parsons, E., Pirani, D., Ashman, R., Daskalopoulou, A., Kerrane, K., McGouran, C., Stevens, L., & Kravets, O. (2021). Manifesting feminist marketing futures: Undertaking a 'visionary' inventory. In P. Maclaran (Ed.), *The Routledge companion to marketing and feminism* (pp. 460–476). Routledge; Sobande, F. (2019). Woke-washing: "Intersectional" femvertising and branding "woke" bravery. *European Journal of Marketing*, *54*(11), 2723–2745. https://doi.org/10.1108/ejm-02-2019-0134.

33 Penniman, A. (2022, June 30). Getting purpose right: Reflections on Cannes Lions 2022. *Medium*. Retrieved October 5, 2022, from https://medium.com/bpi-media/getting-purpose-right-reflections-on-cannes-lions-2022-757c2f27bc82.

34 Ciszek, E., & Logan, N. (2018). Challenging the dialogic promise: How Ben & Jerry's support for Black Lives Matter fosters dissensus on social media. *Journal of Public Relations Research*, *30*(3), 115–127. https://doi.org/10.1080/1062726x.2018.1498342.

35 Duffy, B. E. (2013). Manufacturing authenticity: The rhetoric of "real" in women's magazines. *The Communication Review*, *16*(3), 132–154. https://doi.org/10.1080/10714421.2013.807110.

36 Escalas, J. E., & Bettman, J. R. (2005). Self-construal, reference groups, and brand meaning. *Journal of Consumer Research*, *32*(3), 378–389. https://doi.org/10.1086/497549; Oswald, L. R. (2020). What do affluent Chinese consumers want? A semiotic approach to building brand literacy in developing markets. In L. M. Visconti, P. Lisa, & N. Toulouse (Eds.), *Marketing management: A cultural perspective* (pp. 106–120). Routledge.

37 Lewisohn, C., & Chalfant, H. (2009). *Street art: The graffiti revolution*. Tate Publishing.

38 Cárdenas, D., Castaño, R., Quintanilla, C., & Ayala, E. (2022). Understanding the value of street art for artists, consumers, and brands. *Journal of Current Issues & Research in Advertising, 43*(2), 155–164. https://doi.org/10.1080/10641734.2022.2033652.

39 Baldini, A. L. (2022). What is street art? *Estetika: The European Journal of Aesthetics, LIX/XV*(1), 1–21. https://doi.org/10.33134/eeja.234.

40 Raposo, O. R. (2022). Street art commodification and (an)aesthetic policies on the outskirts of Lisbon. *Journal of Contemporary Ethnography*. https://doi.org/10.1177/08912416221079863.

41 Ferrell, J. (2002). *Tearing down the streets: Adventures in urban anarchy*. Palgrave Macmillan.

42 Stolyarova, A. (2018, October 9). Street art as a tool to urban dialogue. *Street Art Museum*. Retrieved October 6, 2022, from www.streetartmuseumamsterdam.com/post/2018/10/09/street-art-as-a-tool-to-urban-dialogue.

43 Cárdenas, D., Castaño, R., Quintanilla, C., & Ayala, E. (2022). Understanding the value of street art for artists, consumers, and brands. *Journal of Current Issues & Research in Advertising, 43*(2), 155–164. https://doi.org/10.1080/10641734.2022.2033652.

44 Flaherty, J., & Byard, J. (n.d.). How brands are embracing street art to create a new way of talking to consumers post-pandemic. *Creative Moment*. Retrieved October 6, 2022, from www.creativemoment.co/how-brands-are-embracing-street-art-to-create-a-new-way-of-talking-to-consumers-post-pandemic.

45 Droney, D. (2010). The business of "getting up": Street art and marketing in Los Angeles. *Visual Anthropology, 23*(2), 98–114. https://doi.org/10.1080/08949460903472952.

46 Ibid.

47 Trubina, E. (2018). Street art in non-capital urban centres: Between exploiting commercial appeal and expressing social concerns. *Cultural Studies, 32*(5), 676–703. https://doi.org/10.1080/09502386.2018.1429002.

48 Flaherty, J., & Byard, J. (n.d.). How brands are embracing street art to create a new way of talking to consumers post-pandemic. *Creative Moment*. Retrieved October 6, 2022, from www.creativemoment.co/how-brands-are-embracing-street-art-to-create-a-new-way-of-talking-to-consumers-post-pandemic.

49 Droney, D. (2010). The business of "getting up": Street art and marketing in Los Angeles. *Visual Anthropology, 23*(2), 98–114. https://doi.org/10.1080/08949460903472952.

50 Cárdenas, D., Castaño, R., Quintanilla, C., & Ayala, E. (2022). Understanding the value of street art for artists, consumers, and brands. *Journal of Current Issues & Research in Advertising, 43*(2), 155–164. https://doi.org/10.1080/10641734.2022.2033652.

51 Droney, D. (2010). The business of "getting up": Street art and marketing in Los Angeles. *Visual Anthropology, 23*(2), 98–114. https://doi.org/10.1080/08949460903472952.

52 Köroğlu, H. N. (2019). The social construction of the reality via narrative advertising. In *Advances in marketing, customer relationship management, and e-services* (pp. 121–129). https://doi.org/10.4018/978-1-5225-9790-2.ch011.

53 In a sense, street-art advertising executes the idea of détournement, the reuse of preexisting aesthetic elements in such a way as to subvert their original purpose or, in other words, a technique for turning an image or idea against its original intent. By using the aesthetics of advertising against itself, street artists can expose the ideological underpinnings of consumer culture. However, while détournement can be used as a tool for social critique, it can also be appropriated for commercial ends. Debord, G., & Wolman, G. J. (1956). A user's guide to détournement. *libcom.org*. Retrieved October 8, 2022, from https://libcom.org/library/users-guide-d%C3%A9tournement.

54 Lundstrom, K. (2022, July 5). At Cannes, industry critics discuss how the climate crisis fuels Adland's talent wars. *Adweek*. Retrieved October 6, 2022, from www.adweek. com/brand-marketing/cannes-lions-how-climate-crisis-fuels-adlands-talent-wars/.

55 Steurs, G. (1995). Inter-industry R&D spillovers: What difference do they make? *International Journal of Industrial Organization*, *13*(2), 249–276. https://doi. org/10.1016/0167-7187(94)00455-b.

56 Ibid.

57 Nixon, S., & Crewe, B. (2004). Pleasure at work? Gender, consumption and work-based identities in the creative industries. *Consumption Markets & Culture*, *7*(2), 129–147. https://doi.org/10.1080/1025386042000246197.

58 Ibid.

59 Rzepka, C. J. (2017). *Being cool—the work of Elmore Leonard*. Johns Hopkins University Press.

60 Ibid.

61 Holt, D. B. (2002). Why do brands cause trouble? A dialectical theory of consumer culture and branding. *Journal of Consumer Research*, *29*(1), 70–90. https://doi. org/10.1086/339922.

62 Elsbach, K. D., Brown-Saracino, B., & Flynn, F. J. (2015, September 8). Collaborating with creative peers. *Harvard Business Review*. Retrieved October 6, 2022, from https://hbr.org/2015/10/collaborating-with-creative-peers.

63 Beirne, M. (2012). Creative tension? Negotiating the space between the arts and management. *Journal of Arts & Communities*, *4*(3), 149–160. https://doi. org/10.1386/jaac.4.3.149_2.

64 Elsbach, K. D., Brown-Saracino, B., & Flynn, F. J. (2015, September 8). Collaborating with creative peers. *Harvard Business Review*. Retrieved October 6, 2022, from https://hbr.org/2015/10/collaborating-with-creative-peers.

65 Beirne, M. (2012). Creative tension? Negotiating the space between the arts and management. *Journal of Arts & Communities*, *4*(3), 149–160. https://doi. org/10.1386/jaac.4.3.149_2.

66 Ibid.

67 Booker, A. (2021, October 18). Street art pioneer Eric Haze on collaboration, creativity, and China. *Jing Daily*. Retrieved October 8, 2022, from https://jingdaily.com/ qa-street-art-pioneer-eric-haze-on-collaboration-creativity-and-china/.

68 Elsbach, K. D., Brown-Saracino, B., & Flynn, F. J. (2015, September 8). Collaborating with creative peers. *Harvard Business Review*. Retrieved October 6, 2022, from https://hbr.org/2015/10/collaborating-with-creative-peers.

5 Advertising

Regime of paradoxes

> I don't know what it [advertising] means anymore.[1]

> Definitely we are not [just an] advertising agency for quite a while already, creative—yes; ads? Well, it depends, and only to some extent.[2]

> Advertising has a feeling of media that are linear, that are pushy. Can we forget the word advertising, please?[3]

> Let's stop doing advertising.[4]

Advertising has increasingly become an industry where, due to market complexity and an endlessly broadening scope of services,[5] almost nobody knows what *advertising* really is anymore. Nor does anyone want to do "just" advertising. Industry outlets scream about the sector's identity crisis,[6] pointing out that what was "once a creative industry is now a data-driven business reliant on algorithms".[7] They imply the irrelevance of artistry in favor of effectiveness driven by computers, performance marketing, and real-time measurable outcomes. They hint at a potential shift toward a purely economic logic of the industry that takes creativity and cultural production out of the equation. Here, we return to the question of where advertising lies within the creative industries.

In contrast, many practitioners indicate a pressing need for the exact opposite: increasing the focus on developing strategies that deploy the "pull" approach to draw in new audiences in a world dominated by ad blockers and increasing consumer skepticism.[8] As a result, they point to state-of-the-art creativity and cocreation as essential tools for agencies to help brands to get their messages across in today's media environment.

Finally, there are those like New York University Stern School of Business professor Scott Galloway or dentsuACHTUNG's Mervyn Ten Dam, who conclude that we have come to the point where advertising can no longer rescue companies from mediocre products[9] and suggest that many brands should disappear because they bring no value to the users.[10] For creative agencies, this would mean a shift of focus toward supporting brands to enhance their actual value to consumers and, as a result, potentially expanding the business consulting services even further.

DOI: 10.4324/9781003263128-6

Creative industries are full of paradoxes. Precarious working standards, lengthy working hours, limited inclusion and diversity,[11] and a culture of flexibility, self-management, and creativity coexist here.[12] This is also true for advertising. Yet, as much as the sector—in its position as one of the creative industries—is a thorn in the ever-existing conflict between commercial and cultural production, this work invites a more nuanced interpretation of this dichotomy.

Even though the sector is commonly seen as forward-thinking and innovative, allowing for individual talent to develop and thrive in a vibrant creative environment of the agency, it is often only fluid and flexible in appearance.[13] It has become clear that advertising agencies struggle to build new creative cultures that would fit the demands of new generations of creatives while also showing a willingness to learn and borrow from other creative sectors in order to create more engaging and less intrusive advertising. They struggle to adjust internal processes and to find working methods and business models that meet the needs of evolving societies and client–agency relations. Driven by a set of established (and often restrictive) practices and structures on the one hand, and desperately looking to reinvent themselves in a new and more fluid identity befitting today's reality on the other, advertising as a creative industry is a specific *regime of paradoxes*.[14] In other words, the contradictory nature of the advertising industry, where the tension between established practices and the need for fluidity and constant change, results in a struggle to maintain dominant values within the industry while also adapting to changes in society and technology. This results in a constant push and pull between progress and stagnation, leading to challenges in adjusting to changing societal and business realities.

As the term "regime of paradoxes" suggests, the advertising industry is composed of a combination of various paradoxical regimes.[15] In this light, examining regimes of creative effectiveness, artistry, collaboration, and coolness may offer a more nuanced understanding of advertising's position within the creative industries, as they all contribute to the culture-commerce tension that defines the sector. However, these notions have also direct implications for practice; understanding the contradictions within the advertising industry can be a valuable tool for professionals. Examining these regimes allows for deeper insight into how such paradoxes inform the roles, dynamics, and the environment of advertising, and therefore, supports practitioners as they navigate increasingly complex relationships with stakeholders, dynamic creative environments, and cross-sectoral creative processes.

Regime of creative effectiveness

Looking from the legacy perspective, advertising agencies have long operated under the principle that creativity is a service provided to clients—its lifeblood and primary goal[16]—as the agency–client relations were premised on the delivery of creative outputs. In response to changes in the media landscape and the advertising market itself, it has become clear that the advertising industry is undergoing a shift in its understanding and application of creativity.[17] The pressing need for goal orientation and tangible results (as opposed to centering an individual's talent, originality, or artistic mastery) has elevated a *regime of creative effectiveness* within the sector. Even though effectiveness does not always need to be understood as performance marketing and can be associated with brand image work, the treatment of creativity as an instrument for solving client problems and delivering measurable results has become a prevalent discourse in the sector. Some argue that this inevitably leads to the industry's transition from the model of *creativity-as-service* toward the norms of *creativity-as-product* and *results-as-service*.

Supporters of the new model would go as far as suggesting that the industry's preoccupation with artistic expression and delighting audiences leads to neglecting the ultimate goal of achieving tangible outcomes. Ian Leslie describes the tension between creativity and business:

> The ad industry views itself as a field of applied artistry, a next-door neighbor to the entertainment industry. Though it often fails, it aspires to surprise, charm, move and delight people on behalf of its clients. The ad business is obsessed with data science, and distrusts the messy stuff of story, image and idea. The ad industry thinks of itself as the custodian of a brand's meaning in popular culture. The ad business could not care less about such fluff.[18]

The shift, indeed, has potentially significant implications for the way in which agencies do business, from prioritizing measurable outcomes over traditional deliverables and scope-of-work agreements to causing difficulties in proving the value of creativity in their work and convincing clients to approach challenges with a focus on creativity.[19] This could potentially result in a decrease in resources allocated to creative endeavors and difficulties in monetizing the impact of such efforts.

Regime of artistry

Within the advertising industry, there also exists a distinct discourse that we could call a *regime of artistry*. Even though it does not reject the need for a stronger connection between the agency's work and the client's business to create a bigger impact, many experts see creativity as the core power to solve client problems in the face of ad-blocker software, the proliferation of ad-free platforms, and general distrust of advertising, where algorithmic solutions cannot help. In the practitioners' view, advertising needs to change its focus from imposing ads or interrupting audiences' attention to offering actual value in the content that it produces through an engagement with other creative sectors or developing its own (hybrid) genres built around arts or entertainment industry principles.

This view marks a paradigm shift from a focus on *branded* forms (which includes traditional advertising and some branded entertainment) to delivering content coming *from* brands, where brand presence within the cultural products is indirect, implied, or (somewhat) organic and, therefore, not only has a commercial brand-building objective but also artistic ambition.

Through an engagement with other creative sectors, advertising intends to "hide" its commercial character behind the facade of cultural products and embed it in the culture. What emerges through borrowing the tools, aesthetics, and creative practices of other creative industries, but most importantly through the blending of functions, is a "convergent" form of advertising with fluid borders and identity. By blurring the boundaries between "high" and "low" cultural forms, the hyperhybrid[20] form eliminates a visible layer of persuasive meaning and makes audiences identify advertising products as a work of art due to the changed visual poetics.[21] Cannes-winning *5B*, the J&J-sponsored movie, is one such case, which had been applauded by the industry, audiences, and film critics alike.

A *regime of artistry* in advertising, therefore, can be defined as the elevation of aesthetics, creativity, and cultural production within the industry. This ethos goes beyond typical notions of technical proficiency and instead values a more holistic approach to advertising that incorporates artistic expression. The convergence of advertising with other creative industries further reinforces this blurring of boundaries, ultimately inviting a reconsideration of the role of advertising within cultural production.

In this sense, rather than simply serving as a cultural intermediary, advertising is an active player in shaping and contributing to artistic expression, particularly in relation to the increasing prevalence of what Bourdieu terms the "new petite bourgeoisie".[22] However, "struggles over the legitimate definition of culture and the legitimate way of evaluating it"[23] persist, according to Bourdieu.[24] While advertising may attempt to offer viewers experiences that resemble those of other cultural products, it remains fundamentally distinct in its goals. Central to advertising's project is the creation of desires for specific products or services. By contrast, cultural productions typically aim to engage viewers on an emotional or intellectual level, which is now part of the new agenda of an *advertising-as-culture* practice. However, on the contrary, it can be also said that, nowadays, most artists are involved in the creative industries in some way,[25] and the excessive citing of creativity in the discourses of creative industries is not much more than a branding strategy. As Octavi Comeron asks: "What is the aura of an artwork other than 'added value'? . . . Could someone tell a reason to use "creativity" instead of "production" to talk about the kind of labor we do both in art and creative industry?"[26] Others suggest the that "pure" art today is almost nonexistent, as Vito Campanelli argued, "When they [artists] design things that are directed to the market, or rather when they design things that require a communications strategy, a marketing plan, they simply are not making art".[27]

Regime of collaboration

The changing market landscape and approaches to creative work necessitate that advertising agencies invite new skills,[28] and the convergence with other creative sectors asks for different kinds of aesthetic sensibilities.[29] This results in a more visible openness to cooperation, which has further implications for intrasectoral and intersectoral processes and dynamics. *Regime of collaboration*, therefore, marks a change in mindset toward valuing input and ideas from a diverse range of individuals and teams within and outside an agency. This shift challenges the traditional notion of a creative team consisting solely of art directors and copywriters. Instead, there is recognition that insight and inspiration may come from broader cocreation, and ideas can be sourced from various individuals within an agency, as well as external experts with specific skillsets. As was the case of Next Rembrandt, in which specialists from various sectors together innovated and delivered a new kind of value for the brand. Agencies also involve their clients more in the creative process and treat them as a partner.

In addition, the regime of collaboration manifests itself through looking toward other creative industries for innovative (to advertising) approaches to cocreation, as in the instance of the writers' room model, implemented by some agencies developing entertainment-style campaigns. There is an indication that advertising will continue to look toward the creative practices of the entertainment industry, as the incorporation of artistic practices into management strategies proves to invigorate and empower work teams. These initiatives can improve learning and promote employee adaptability, improvisation, and creativity—integral elements in the contemporary knowledge economy.[30]

The shift toward increased collaboration, especially intrasectoral, affects the power dynamics of creative processes and does not come without its challenges. Even though collaborative efforts, in general, are premised upon shared risk, shared responsibility, shared resources, and shared rewards, as discussed by Himmelman,[31] examining the power dynamics of collaboration between the advertising industry and other creative sectors illustrates the hierarchies and unequal distribution of resources that exist in agency-led projects. While agencies may have access to clients and, therefore, control over budgets and decision-making processes, artists and entertainment professionals often have a distinct artistic vision or expertise that is necessary for the project's success. This power imbalance can lead to issues of creative ownership and artistic freedom, as agencies may lack answerability to their collaborators, while they hold a significant amount of power in shaping cultural production.

Seeking a regime of cool

"Cool is a slang word connoting a certain style that involves masking and hiding emotions. What was once a low-profile means of survival and later a youthful rebellious alternative to class-based status systems has become commoditized".[32] The concept of "coolness" in advertising is not a novel idea. Previous research shows that a brand's perception of being cool is significant for consumer decision-making[33] and is often associated with the perception of being "hip and trendy".[34] Advertisers may attempt to tap into this by positioning promoted products and services as aligned with cultural trends or appealing to a specific subcultural group.[35]

However, the applicability of "coolness" in relation to the advertising industry is multilayered. On the one hand, the attempt to hide advertising's persuasiveness behind a façade of cultural products[36] can be seen as a *strategy of coolness*. Since as Douglas Holt explains: "to be authentic, brands must be disinterested; they must be perceived as invented and disseminated by parties without an instrumental economic agenda, by people who are intrinsically motivated by their inherent value".[37] Yet, at the same time, while there is no guarantee that highly creative advertising will make it more memorable or appealing to consumers,[38] research has shown that consumer perceptions of creativity in advertising can positively impact the brand.[39] In other words, even if the creative effort may initially appear to be "wasted",[40] it can serve as a signal of effort and "brand fitness" to potential consumers.[41] Therefore, by incorporating the genres and aesthetics of other creative industries into advertising campaigns, brands may convey their inherent values more authentically while also appealing to consumers through creativity and innovation. At the same time, they may signal a sense of cultural relevance and connectedness, potentially further improving brand image and consumer perception.

Looking from another perspective, advertising desperately needs to find its "new-cool" as an employer to retain and attract talent. In light of what appears to be an image crisis, the advertising industry must remain competitive in its pursuit of creative talent. One way to reposition itself in the eyes of the youth is through involvement in innovative or socially engaged projects and cross-sectoral collaborations with industries that currently appear "cool" or culturally significant. As cultural intermediaries, advertising practitioners are not necessarily limited to mediating between producers and consumers or directing cultural change.[42] However, involvement in highly creative projects involving the production of (popular) culture can also fulfill the personal aspirations and ambitions of creative professionals, demonstrating the potential for success in the industry. Advertising, therefore, offers a promise of feeding the "taste for trendy" as Taylor points out,[43] or proving (by delivering highly innovative projects), as Korsten specifies, that "anything is possible".

Notes

1 J. Grossberg, personal communication, April 20, 2022.
2 COO of independent creative agency, personal communication, February 2, 2022.
3 M. Ten Dam, personal communication, January 10, 2022.

4 CCO of network agency, personal communication, January 14, 2022.

5 Kumar, V., & Gupta, S. (2016). Conceptualizing the evolution and future of advertising. *Journal of Advertising*, *45*(3), 302–317. https://doi.org/10.1080/00913367.2 016.1199335; Schultz, D. (2016). The future of advertising or whatever we're going to call it. *Journal of Advertising*, *45*(3), 276–285. https://doi.org/10.1080/00913367 .2016.1185061.

6 For example: Banham, M. (2022, January 31). Advertising's identity crisis and the demise of the third-party cookie. *Amobee*. Retrieved October 16, 2022, from www.amobee.com/blog/advertisings-identity-crisis-and-the-demise-of-the-third-party-cookie/; Leslie, I. (2018, August 9). RIP Don Draper: How algorithms killed the advertising creative. *Australian Financial Review*. Retrieved October 16, 2022, from www.afr.com/companies/media-and-marketing/who-killed-don-draper-advertising-in-the-age-of-google-and-facebook-20180806-h13lnm; Nottmeier, K. (2018, November 29). Is advertising experiencing an identity crisis? *DMEXCO*. Retrieved October 16, 2022, from https://dmexco.com/stories/ is-advertising-experiencing-an-identity-crisis/.

7 Leslie, I. (2018, August 9). Rip Don Draper: How algorithms killed the advertising creative. *Australian Financial Review*. Retrieved October 16, 2022, from www.afr. com/companies/media-and-marketing/who-killed-don-draper-advertising-in-the-age-of-google-and-facebook-20180806-h13lnm.

8 "Pull" strategies as engagement tactics that have grown to be significant in 2000s.

9 Siva, L. (2017, January 30). Scott Galloway: Death of the advertising industrial complex. *Nordic Business Forum*. Retrieved October 16, 2022, from www.nbforum. com/nbreport/scott-galloway-death-advertising-industrial-complex/.

10 M. Ten Dam, personal communication, January 10, 2022.

11 Brook, O., O'Brien, D., & Taylor, M. (2020). *Culture is bad for you: Inequality in the cultural and creative industries*. Manchester University Press.

12 Villela Garcia, M., & Willatt, A. (2021, October 18). Creative industry paradoxes: New business models and spaces of change. *Policy Bristol Hub*. Retrieved October 16, 2022, from https://policybristol.blogs.bris.ac.uk/category/research/ business-economic-policy/.

13 Lynch, J. (2019). Advertising industry evolution: Agency creativity, fluid teams and diversity. An exploratory investigation. *Journal of Marketing Management*, *35*(9– 10), 845–866. https://doi.org/10.1080/0267257x.2019.1635188.

14 The term "regime of paradoxes", used here in relation to today's advertising, is loosely inspired by Foucault's concept of "regimes of truth." Foucault suggests that power structures shape what is considered to be "truth"; that truth "is produced by virtue of multiple constraints and it induces regulated effects of power" and "each society has its regime of truth." This idea is transplanted to the work of this book in the sense that the production of knowledge within creative industries, specifically advertising, is driven by a constant push for creativity and innovation, but at the same time, those are restricted by multiple factors like in-agency structures, time constraints, or the push for measurable effectives, just to name a few. Foucault, M. (2020). *Discipline and punish: The birth of the prison*. Penguin Classics.

15 It is important to mention that this series of paradoxes relates only to the core scope of this research—namely the exploration of advertising's place within the creative industries—and by no means exhausts the complexity of the sector or take into consideration all the paradoxes existing therein.

16 Lynch, J. (2019). Advertising industry evolution: Agency creativity, fluid teams and diversity. An exploratory investigation. *Journal of Marketing Management*, *35*(9–10), 845–866. https://doi.org/10.1080/0267257x.2019.1635188; Koslow, S., Sasser, S. L., & Riordan, E. A. (2003). What is creative to whom and why? *Journal of Advertising Research*, *43*(1), 96–110. https://doi.org/10.2501/jar-43-1-96-110.

17 Even though creativity and innovation need to be understood as separate and distinctive concepts, when it comes to the dynamics affecting their comprehension and operationalization within the advertising industry, the logics and issues becomes similar. Hence, the impact of creativity and innovation are merged when understood as newness within innovation.
18 Leslie, I. (2018, August 9). Rip Don Draper: How algorithms killed the advertising creative. *Australian Financial Review*. Retrieved October 16, 2022, from www.afr. com/companies/media-and-marketing/who-killed-don-draper-advertising-in-the-age-of-google-and-facebook-20180806-h13lnm.
19 For example: Cannes Lions. (2022). (rep.). *State of creativity 2022*. Cannes Lions; Kübler, R. V., & Proppe, D. (2012). Faking or convincing: Why do some advertising campaigns win creativity awards? *Business Research*, *5*(1), 60–81. https:// doi.org/10.1007/bf03342732; Hurman, J. (2016). *The case for creativity: The link between imaginative marketing & commercial success*. Cannes Lions.
20 Szczęsna, E. (2004). *Tożsamość hybrydyczna*. ER(R)GO: Teoria-Literatura-Kultura. Retrieved October 16, 2022, from http://cejsh.icm.edu.pl/cejsh/element/bwmeta1. element.ojs-issn-2544-3186-year-2004-issue-9-article-2344.
21 Wywioł, A. (2019, March 18). *Współczesne strategie w poetyce reklamy jako wyznaczniki jej możliwej autonomiczności. Próba ujęcia krytycznego*. Uniwersytet Pedagogiczny w Krakowie.
22 According to Bourdieu, the new petite bourgeoisie is a broad social group made up of young, credentialized actors who create wants, and those who "play a vanguard role in the struggles over everything concerned with the art of living, in particular, domestic life and consumption." Bourdieu, P. (1989). *Distinction a social critique of the judgement of taste*. Routledge.
23 Ibid.
24 Taylor, T. D. (2009). Advertising and the conquest of culture. *Social Semiotics*, *19*(4), 405–425. https://doi.org/10.1080/10350330903361091.
25 Lovink, G., & Rossiter, N. (2007). *MyCreativity reader: A critique of creative industries*. Institute of Network Cultures.
26 Ibid.
27 Ibid.
28 Lynch, J. (2019). Advertising industry evolution: Agency creativity, fluid teams and diversity. An exploratory investigation. *Journal of Marketing Management*, *35*(9–10), 845–866. https://doi.org/10.1080/0267257x.2019.1635188.
29 Wywioł, A. (2019, March 18). *Współczesne strategie w poetyce reklamy jako wyznaczniki jej możliwej autonomiczności. Próba ujęcia krytycznego*. Uniwersytet Pedagogiczny w Krakowie.
30 Beirne, M. (2012). Creative tension? Negotiating the space between the arts and management. *Journal of Arts & Communities*, *4*(3), 149–160. https://doi.org/10.1386/jaac.4.3.149_2.
31 Himmelman, A. T. (2015). *The four shared RS of collaboration*. Himmelman Consulting.
32 Belk, R. W., Tian, K., & Paavola, H. (2010). Consuming cool: Behind the unemotional mask. *Research in Consumer Behavior*, 183–208. https://doi.org/10.1108/s0885-2111(2010)0000012010.
33 Budzanowski, A. (2017). *Why coolness should matter to marketing and when consumers desire a cool brand: An examination of the impact and limit to the perception of brand coolness* (dissertation). University of St. Gallen, School of Management, Economics, Law, Social Sciences, and International Affairs, St. Gallen, Switzerland.
34 Belk, R. W., Tian, K., & Paavola, H. (2010). Consuming cool: Behind the unemotional mask. *Research in Consumer Behavior*, 183–208. https://doi.org/10.1108/s0885-2111(2010)0000012010.

35 Ibid.
36 Similarly to the execution of guerrilla, or what some would call "under-the-radar" marketing, utilization of user-generated content, viral marketing or product placement. Serazio, M. (2013). *Your ad here: The cool sell of guerrilla marketing.* New York University Press; Bond, J., & Kirshenbaum, R. (1998). *Under the radar: Talking to today's cynical consumer.* Wiley; Shrum, L. J. (2017). *The psychology of entertainment media: Blurring the lines between entertainment and persuasion.* Routledge.
37 Holt, D. B. (2002). Why do brands cause trouble? A dialectical theory of consumer culture and branding. *Journal of Consumer Research, 29*(1), 70–90. https://doi.org/10.1086/339922.
38 Kover, A. J., Goldberg, S. M., & James, W. L. (1995). Creativity vs. effectiveness? An integrating classification for advertising. *Journal of Advertising Research, 35*(6).
39 Dahlén, M., Rosengren, S., & Törn, F. (2008). Advertising creativity matters. *Journal of Advertising Research, 48*(3), 392–403. https://doi.org/10.2501/s002184990808046x.
40 Kover, A. J., Goldberg, S. M., & James, W. L. (1995). Creativity vs. effectiveness? An integrating classification for advertising. *Journal of Advertising Research, 35*(6).
41 Ambler, T., & Hollier, E. A. (2004). The waste in advertising is the part that works. *Journal of Advertising Research, 44*(4), 375–389. https://doi.org/10.1017/s0021849904040413.
42 Taylor, T. D. (2009). Advertising and the conquest of culture. *Social Semiotics, 19*(4), 405–425. https://doi.org/10.1080/10350330903361091.
43 Ibid.

Index

5b 1, 56–57, 59, 84

Academy Award 1, 61
Accenture 22
adidas 18
Adorno, Theodor 9
advertising: appropriating 72; -as-culture 84
advertising agency *see* creative, agency
Anderson, Matt 17
art directors 8, 33, 60, 85
artificial intelligence 31
artistry 4, 6, 39, 53, 68–69, 71–72, 74–76, 81–85
arts, subversive 71–72
audiences 2–3, 10, 14, 18, 20, 34, 50–55, 58–59, 67–68, 71–72, 75, 84

Beam Suntory 25
Ben & Jerry 9, 69, 71
Blandon, Loren 25
BMW 54
Bourdieu, Pierre 84
brand: attitudes 5, 40; building 18, 37; entertainment 57–58; purpose film 56–57, 59
Brändärit 52
branded entertainment 6, 19, 52–55, 57, 84
budgets, advertising 19–20, 37, 44, 63, 85
business models 17, 20–21, 62, 82
Byard, James 71–72

Campanelli, Vito 84
can-do-better attitude 41
Cannes Lions 1, 4, 23, 39, 41, 55, 70, 84
Chipotle 53
Clayton, Steve 16

client relations 15, 17, 23, 40, 62, 82
clients, risk-averse 63
cocreation 59–62, 68, 75–76, 81, 85
Colamarino, Sarah 56
Colenso BBDO 18
collaboration 6, 59–62, 69, 71, 74–76, 82, 85; cross-sectoral 4, 6, 60–61, 73, 86
Comeron, Octavi 84
consumer: behavior 9, 18, 70; engagement 18, 23, 53
consumerism 67, 71
coolness 24, 72–74, 82, 85–86
Cooper, James 25
copywriters 8–9, 16, 33, 60–61, 85
crafts 13, 15–16, 56
creative: agency 1–5, 9–10, 14–25, 31, 33–36, 38–45, 51–52, 55, 57–63, 70, 72–76, 81–83, 85; control 24, 61–62, 76, 85; culture 4–5, 82; industries 2–9, 13, 34, 37, 45, 68, 81–82, 84–86; processes 3, 6, 34–35, 52, 55, 57, 59–60, 62, 74–75, 82, 85
creative teams, managing 4–5, 21, 31, 33, 38, 40, 45, 60–61, 63, 85
creativity 1, 3, 5–7, 9, 13–18, 21–24, 33–34, 39, 41–42, 61, 73, 75, 81–86; awards 15–16, 36, 40, 42; monetization 4, 7; as problem solving 13–14, 41; -as-product 15, 83; as seed of innovation 34; -as-service 15–16, 83
Credle, Susan 23–24
Csikszentmihalyi, Mihaly 24
cultural: intermediaries 10, 19, 84, 86; production 7, 9, 68, 81–82, 84–85; products 2–3, 9, 34, 74, 84, 86
Curt, Lionel 60, 76

DCMS (Department of Culture, Media and Sport) 6–7, 9
dentsuACHTUNG 38, 54, 81
disinterest 42, 74
Displaced 37
documentaries 1–2, 25, 55–57
Dove 9, 53
Droga5 22
Droney, Damien 72
Drucker, Peter 33

economy: creative 6, 8; experience 67–68, 72
effectiveness, creative 2, 15, 18, 40, 50, 81–83
entertainment 2–5, 13, 51–52, 54–55, 57, 60–61, 63, 68, 72, 85; brand-sponsored 6, 19, 56–57, 62, 84

FCB 23
Flaherty, John 71–72
fluidity 6, 82
freedom, creative 23–24, 44, 51, 62, 73
Futerra 73

Galloway, Scott 81
Gardner, Howard 24
genres, hybrid 2, 9, 52, 67
Goodman, Jae 38, 53–55, 60–61
great resignation 24, 74
Grossberg, Josh 13, 20–23

Hall, Bruce 18
Haze, Eric 76
hip consumerism 69–70
Hirshberg, Eric 15
Hollywood 6, 9, 53, 55–57, 60, 63
Holt, Douglas 74, 86
Horkheimer, Max 9
Hurman, James 18

identity, creative 42, 75
ING 31, 38
innovation 3, 5, 7, 24, 31, 33–36, 38, 40–45, 59, 73, 86; as application of creativity 34, 83

Johnson & Johnson 56, 59

Kendall, Nick 35
Korsten, Bas 31, 33, 37–38, 42, 44, 63, 86

Langton, Pat 16
Lash, Scott 10
Last Ever Issue 40
Lego 52–53
Lego Movie 52
Leslie, Ian 83
Lury, Celia 10

Maconick, Rupert 57, 59, 62–63
McCann 13, 16
media: agencies 19–20, 58; planning 19–20, 58; pull 2, 81; push 2, 50, 81; traditional 2, 20, 50–51, 56–57, 59, 72
Method, Marcus 74
MNSTR 61

Narayanan, Nikhil 25
narratives 50, 54, 68
Netflix 59, 68
New York Times 37–38
Next Rembrandt 31–33, 37–38, 42, 73, 85
Nike 9, 17

Observatory Agency 53–54, 59–60
Odendaal, Pierre 16

Pilkington, Andy 18
popular culture 10, 61, 83
power imbalance 85
production: process 40, 57; studio 51, 60, 62–63
product placement 51, 54, 56

Raunio, Juha-Matti 52
Ray, Bob 22
Real Beauty Sketches 53
Red Bull 2, 53
regime: of artistry 83–84; of collaboration 85; of cool 86; of paradoxes 6, 81–82
responsibility 20, 43, 62, 75
results-as-service 16, 83
Rijksmuseum 31, 38
Road Tales 39

Shields-Shimizu, Brendan 59
Sinclair, John 9
social issues 6, 68–70
Spence, Jessica 25
Stefanidou, Nicoletta 22
Steurs, Geert 73
storytelling 6, 33, 39, 50, 52–60, 83

street art 71–72, 76
Szczepaniak, Dawid 15, 36, 39–41, 45, 70, 73

talent crisis 4, 23–25, 42, 45, 72–74, 83, 86
TBWA 52
Ten Dam, Mervyn 38–39, 54, 81
Thorsby, David 8
Tinker Tailor 22
Townsend, Solitaire 73

virtual reality 37–38
VMLY&R 15, 25, 40
Volkswagen 38–39

Warhol, Andy 67
Wiese, Mike 50, 55, 61–62
Wójcik, Julita 69
woke-washing 69–70
Work Foundation 8
writers' room 60, 85
Wunderman Thompson 31–32

Printed in the United States
by Baker & Taylor Publisher Services